What Authors are Saying about

Writing From the Inside Out...

"Great job! *Writing From the Inside Out* will certainly be a helpful tool for lots of people. I've shown it to a number of my clients and students."

— Hal Zina Bennett
author, *Write From the Heart: Unleashing the Power of Your Creativity*

"Your wonderful book is inspiring and informative. I especially liked the way you integrated psychological exploration into your journal exercises."

—Elizabeth Fishel
author, *Sisters* and
*Reunion: The Girls We Used To Be,
The Women We Become*

"*Writing From the Inside Out* offers a wealth of ways to embark on your journey of self-discovery. Whether you've kept a journal before or want to start now, you'll find techniques and tips in this book that will help you discover who you are—and become who you were meant to be."

—Margot Silk Forrest
author, *A Short Course in Kindness*

"If you'd like to get unstuck in your life and enjoy a greater flow of creativity, read Susan Borkin's books. Gently and wisely the exercises and commentary facilitate your self-awareness and growth. Inspiring!"

—Marcia Yudkin
author, *Freelance Writing for Magazines
& Newspapers* and 10 other books

What Therapists are Saying about

Writing From the Inside Out...

"This book gives my clients the hands-on, practical tools they need for sustained, in-depth journaling. It is helpful not only during the therapeutic process but also for continuing growth and transformation."

— Pamela Bjorklund, Ph.D.
Psychologist

"I am impressed! This book is full of good ideas, direction and belief in the individual."

—Amy Wallerstein Friedman
Licensed Clinical Social Worker

"I found this book packed full of new ideas that lead to powerful insights and the release of blocked energy. As a psychotherapist, I highly recommend this book to my clients. It also stimulated me to return to journal writing for myself."

—Lynn Kennedy
Licensed Marriage & Family Therapist

"*Writing From the Inside Out* is a product of a long and thoughtful personal discovery of authenticity. Each page reflects the author's creativity, humor and practical approach to the struggles and joys of getting to know yourself from the *inside out*. Susan Borkin's discipline, energy, focus, dedication and integrity shine through this very helpful and reader-friendly book."

— Patrice Otten
Licensed Clinical Social Worker

Writing
From the
Inside Out

Using a Journal for
Personal Growth & Transformation

Susan Borkin, M.A.

Center for Personal Growth and Development • Los Altos, California

In loving memory of my mother
Marion Borkin

Author's Note:

Confidentiality of my clients and workshop participants is of the highest priority. To that end, all examples and case histories are used with permission, only.

This book is designed for personal growth. It is not intended or able to provide mental health care. If you experience symptoms that may require such care, please seek the services of a qualified, licensed, mental health practitioner or psychotherapist.

Library of Congress Catalog Card Number: 94-93956

ISBN: 0-9644897-0-8

Cover Illustration: Vicki Brink
Cover Design: Kim Moeller
Photo Credit: Dave Lepori

Center for Personal Growth and Development
P.O. Box 1615
Los Altos, CA 94023-1615
(800) 552-9748

Acknowledgments

I'd like to thank members of my Graduate Committee, Peter Pursley and Pat Henry from the former Lone Mountain College in San Francisco, California, for consenting to accept my original thesis "Journal Writing as Self-Therapy" in 1977.

I'd like to acknowledge the contributions of several fine teachers and trainers of the gestalt therapy process, Lois Llewellyn, Lou Pambianco and Lu Grey.

I'd like to thank Elizabeth Fishel for creating a great model for a journal writing support group in Berkeley, California, years ago.

I wish to thank my former colleagues at the Almaden Institute in San Jose, California, especially Sue Fairey for encouraging me and supporting my efforts to expand my Journal Writing for Personal Growth Workshops in the San Jose and South Bay area. And thanks to my bi-weekly support and granola group, Marcia Kaufmann, Rosemarie Guasconi, and Diane Petroni-Newhouse.

To Ann Stevenson for providing giggles and on-going phone and voicemail support. To Peggy Keelin for being the original midwife at the envisioning stage of this book.

Heartfelt thanks to: My friends of many, many years, Marla Rosner and Perviz Randeria for listening so long to the ups and downs of this process; Judy Mize and Sharie Todd, dear friends to the south and north, although distant geographically, close to my heart in spirit; and Jackie Payne and Ann Getzoff, for suggestions and feedback along the way. Special thanks to my sister, Donna Borkin, for long distance coaching and feedback.

For their loving support, blessings, and feedback, warm thanks to my women's group, Marcia Pugsley, Patrice Otten, Eileen Sanchez, Pam Bjorklund, and Faye Livingston-Kimura.

I would like to thank my husband Jerry Hurwitz for, in his own loving way, pushing me when I insisted years ago, "No one will buy this stuff" and for hours of endless nighttime listening with eyes just barely open.

To Georgia Dow, a truly gentle, nurturing and healing soul to me, for providing retreat time at the Nest, helping me to see the Big Picture and for being a witness to my ongoing growth process.

And I would like to thank Larissa Keet for being a later midwife in my life, confidant and friend during my continuing movement, progress and personal growth on this project. And for the acknowledgment that the book is already done, I just hadn't written it down yet.

To my virtual publishing company: Marti Ainsworth for firm and clear copy editing; Vicki Brink for fine illustrations and cover art; Charles Chickadel for his kindness, support, nuts and bolts feedback, and guidance through the publishing and printing world; and Kim Moeller, who saw and believed the vision early on and who provided support, graphic and formatting skills in an effort to help me look good on paper.

Contents

Part I
Beginning the Inner Journey

Chapter One

What's In It For You...
How This Book Can Change Your Life

*Awareness is a tool and if you are aware, then you have
choices. The more awareness you have, the more you
pick and choose; the more choices you can make.*
Jim Simkin

"How This Book Can Change Your Life." Quite a claim with
over 50,000 books published a year! So what's in it for you?
Will using a personal journal double your income? Help you
lose that extra ten pounds? Find your ideal mate? Will it improve your sex life or find you a perfect job?

> **Jim** found that by keeping a log of his sales calls, he
> could see customer patterns, correct weaknesses in
> his presentation, and give himself vital pep "talks"
> throughout the day. His narrative log became an
> essential tool for increasing his income.

> **Ellen** had struggled with an extra stubborn ten
> pounds for years. It wasn't until she began writing

about her weight loss efforts that she was able to keep those pounds off permanently. By recording her food log, noting details of her workout and exercise plan, and writing about her feelings during her weight loss, Ellen was able to get in touch with the underlying issues of her weight challenge.

Nina had fantasized about her ideal mate for years. When she learned to write affirmations about her ideal relationship, she also broke through the blocks that had sabotaged her relationships in the past. By focusing on what she wanted and releasing her unconscious negative beliefs on paper, Nina began to draw suitable partners into her life.

Ben was in a good relationship. He was deeply in love with his wife, but felt less than satisfied with the level of their intimacy. By using dialogues and clarifying his needs on paper, Ben was able to ask specifically for what he wanted and needed. His clarity helped his wife express her needs as well. Both Ben and his wife learned a mutual letter writing technique, which helped them to communicate more directly and openly with one another.

Stephanie knew she was unhappy at work, but didn't know what she wanted to be doing. By using visualization and recording what she envisioned, Stephanie began to create a picture of herself working in a more comfortable environment. Combining visualization with techniques for recording her dreams, Stephanie realized the true direction of her life work.

You can change and heal your life in 3 basic steps.

Journal writing offers you steps to make these kind of changes in *your* life. *Writing From the Inside Out* is all about growth, healing, and changing your life for the better. In just three steps you can become more self-aware, discover new and healthier options, and create the changes you desire.

The personal journal is your writer-friendly tool in this simple, but powerful life-changing process. If life-changing sounds extreme, consider this: When you begin journal writing on a regular basis, or once you simply write your first entry, you'll find yourself embarking on a journey of self-discovery and transformation.

You will learn that the process of personal journal writing is different from the way you have been taught writing before. No red pens to correct misspelled words or punctuation. No rigidly structured format or rules to follow. Journal writing is focused on the process, on the journey of discovery itself, not the outcome. What you find out about yourself, what you learn in the process of writing is much more important than the finished product. Journal writing is a process that uses writing to grow and heal from the inside out. Growth and healing begin by writing from your own personal awareness, without editing, without interruption, without interpretation.

Writing From the Inside Out is like an atlas, but instead of road maps, the maps you will be given are about your inner journey. These maps and guidelines reflect numerous ways to increase your internal awareness, the place where personal growth and transformation begin.

What Does Awareness Do For You?

This free-flow, rule-less style of journal writing provides you with options you might have missed in a more structured experience. The lack of structure allows more room to explore options, and therein lies its power. Growth, change and healing begin with awareness. This awareness and the freedom to write without restraint give you options. Options give you choices.

How Does This Process Work?

The process of writing from the inside out works by first becoming aware of your current situation. Let's start with an example.

You come home from work on Friday night. You're exhausted from the week, and want nothing more to do than turn on TV, and scrounge through the refrigerator for some leftover pizza. You glance quickly at the mail and see only bills and advertisements. You start thinking another week has gone by and you're still in a dead-end job. You feel caught, staying where you are to make ends meet. You keep up the mortgage on your home or the rent on your apartment. You make your car payments, earning just enough money to survive, but not enough to get ahead. You get by, keep your head above water, but can't reach the shore. You're stuck.

To Begin Writing, Start With a Sensation or Feeling

To begin your first writing exercise, you may start with a physical sensation, a feeling, an awareness, a thought, or whatever you are first conscious of. As this beginning awareness grows and deepens, you will begin to notice other things around you. Your awareness will expand to see other perspectives and possibilities. Automatically, your options will increase. Increasing options gives you choices previously unnoticed. Choices allow you to creatively make change.

Stop for a minute. Look around you. Close your eyes. Allow yourself to become quiet. Let your breathing slow and your body relax. Now imagine what you'd like to be doing. You'll want to edit, but don't. Let your fantasy run wild without interruption or interpretation. Fill in all the details of what you'd like to be doing.

You might start with the visual details: What do you look like? What do your surroundings look like? What do you see going on around you? Then try the kinesthetic details: What are you doing? What do you feel like? What is going on around you? Finally, still quiet, eyes closed, listen for a minute. Notice the sounds around you. Do you hear a breeze rippling through leaves? Do you hear tropical music, birds calling overhead?

Get as clear a picture, a sense and sound as possible. Before you edit this scene, quickly pick up your pen and write it down. All of it. All the details. Leave nothing out. Go! Write your fantasy on the next page:

**Stop &
Write**

_____

_____

_____

_____

_____

_____

_____

_____

_____

_____

_____

_____

You've written it out, but your internal critic gets back early from lunch. "What is the meaning of this daydreaming?" it asks. "How dare you be idly fantasizing instead of working? How dare you escape when you need to be busy at your work?"

But hold on a minute here. Let's look again. Re-read your fantasy. Re-read it again, carefully this time. Before chucking the whole thing, have a look at it. It may seem far-fetched, but what are the essential qualities your fantasy has captured? More freedom? Being outdoors? More space? More open-endedness? More time?

Before you rip this page out of the book, turn to the next page. Quickly write out five things you could do that would connect the fantasy with what you are envisioning as your current reality. Write down small things, things that would take little or no effort. Write down five things you could do now or within the next day or so. Could you bring a green plant into your workspace, or put up a poster of a tropical island on a blank wall? Could you check on your comp time or accumulated vacation days? Could you call a travel agent and check on specials to Hawaii or the local community college's travel courses? Go wild! Let yourself explore every possibility. Write out at least five things you can do within a few days:

Stop & Write

1. _____
2. _____
3. _____
4. _____
5. _____

Go back and read your original fantasy one more time. What else is it telling you about what you want or need in your life that you're missing now? More time with your family? More time alone? More time to just sit and meditate or read? More pleasure from the day–to–day routine of your work?

Write out five more things that meet your needs in the next day or week. Write quickly, without editing. Again, keep the changes small and manageable, but write them down:

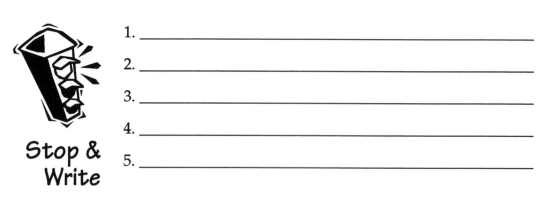

Stop & Write

1. _____
2. _____
3. _____
4. _____
5. _____

You don't have to restructure your entire life, but you now have a list that will move you closer to the essence of your fantasy with very little effort. Imagine doing this type of exercise everyday! It really is an exercise, because like exercise you do with your body, this emotional and mental innerwork exercise also stretches you. It moves you closer to where you want to be. It stretches your inside muscles.

So how did you get here? You stopped, quieted down, looked around and listened. Then you went one step further. You looked at what you were missing, at what else you wanted. The simple slowing down and checking in, the one more step to writing it down, is the essence of keeping a personal journal. So what have you got? You now have a record of your own thinking process. You have increased your awareness, you have more focus and greater clarity. You also have at least a ten-item "things to do list," ready to go.

Slow down, check in, write it down: the essence of journal keeping

Do you see how simply increasing your awareness, turning your attention inward, and recording what you notice is the bridge connecting you to the second step—discovering options? As you pay more attention to yourself, the discovery of options and choices for a better way occurs automatically. These are your new options. Now, look again at your ten-item list.

Not all of the items will work. Some are highly impractical and some do not seem possible right now. But there is something on that list that will provide you with the kernel for the third and final step. You are now able to review your options and create change. *To create change, you must first become aware and then have specific options to explore.*

Now, look at your written fantasy again. Has your perspective changed at all in this process? Do things look or feel differently now? What was your inner self trying to tell you? What are the essential qualities missing in your life right now? What would you like to be different? What things can you take control of and change? What do you want and need to do next? Look again at your "to do" list. Add to it. Change it. Cross out what doesn't fit.

Now for the final step. You have become aware of your current reality, conscious of the deepest sense of what you want and need. You have discovered a whole list of options for yourself. Your options have substance and depth. Now it's time to choose. Now it's time to create change. But now you are armed with focus, purpose and a sense of inner direction.

Let's review the process. To make it even easier, think of it as simply as the ABC's.

The steps are as basic as ABC!

Awareness begins the process:
1. Find a quiet, uninterrupted time alone.
2. Let your breathing slow and deepen.
3. Notice where you are holding tension.
4. Pay attention to your feelings, body sensations, visions, thoughts.

Broaden your options and possibilities:
1. Remain quiet, allowing your breathing to continue to deepen.
2. Let any images, pictures, sounds and feelings float freely without restraint.
3. Write down all the sensations you notice.
4. Allow the sensations to change and shift. Write these down as well.

Create change based on your new awareness:
1. Ask yourself, what do you know now that you didn't know when you began this exercise?
2. With this new information, what would you like to do right now? What new ideas do you have for doing something differently a little later?
3. Continue with this process as long as you wish, moving back and forth between awareness, expanding awareness, and recording what you notice.
4. Review what you've written and change what would be most useful for you.

Throughout this book, many additional methods will be used. Each will begin with a brief period of quiet, allowing your current awareness to surface. Growth and transformation begin on this journey, the process of writing from the inside out.

Chapter Two

Logistics and Equipment...
Pack Your Bag With Tools of the Trade

I have at last got the little room I have wanted so long,
and am very happy about it. It does me good to be alone.
Louisa May Alcott

Journal writing is a solitary process. You may be writing in your journal within the context of a group or workshop, but the exploration created by the journal is essentially done alone. To get both the greatest value and enjoyment from your journal writing time, there are several guidelines you'll want to consider. This chapter presents ideas to support the logistics or time and space elements of using your personal journal. In addition, it will address the selection of equipment and tools for future journal writing.

When and Where to Use Your Journal

Keshia came in to see me two weeks after a journal writing workshop. She told me it was difficult for her to get to her journal. Each day following the workshop she had the best

Write When
Your Energy
is High

intentions to sit down and write. She started each day with her motivation high, but when late evening came and the house was finally quiet, she was simply too exhausted to sit down and write. The later it got in the day, the busier she became. Keshia remembered that in college, she had formed a habit of getting up very early in the morning to finish writing papers she had been completely blocked on the night before. By getting to bed just a little earlier, Keshia was able to get up earlier in the morning to a quiet household. She not only found it easier to get to her journal writing at this time of day, but found herself actually looking forward to the solitude.

Ginny had just the opposite problem. She seemed to wake up and get going about 3:00 in the afternoon. Ginny found her most creative time at about 10:00 pm. By 10:30 pm, Ginny told me she was just "warming up" and wrote several lengthy in-depth journal entries.

Neither Keshia's nor Ginny's situation is right or wrong for everyone. You will need to experiment to find the right time of day. If you have flexibility in your schedule, you can also write during a lunch hour or afternoon break. The trick is, to find your best energy time and establish a regular writing habit. You can of course, write any time you feel like writing. But by establishing a regular habit you will find that you will want to write more frequently at other times as well.

Write Where You Won't Be Disturbed

Once you have established the time you will do your journal writing, find a place where you will not be interrupted. Set up your writing environment to please yourself. If you need to share the space with others, try to negotiate a time that you will have the space to yourself, uninterrupted.

Write Where You're Comfortable

The place you select for writing in your journal should be well-lit, (at least light enough to see your paper), and well ventilated. Make it aesthetic and pleasant. Bring in favorite objects, posters, or knickknacks. Frame a meaningful quotation. You might even look beyond the usual writing places, like a desk or office and seek out a unique place. Consider writing under a tree, in a loft, or near a stream. Be creative and open to new possibilities.

Cari told me she got her husband and teenagers off to work and school in the morning, made herself a fresh pot of tea and climbed back into bed to write. Cari called this spot her "nest," with large pillows propped up, a bed tray for her tea, and a lap desk to write on. She arrived at work late morning and returned home later in the evening than the rest of her family. Cari used her morning time for herself and found her own bed to be the most comfortable spot to write.

David told me he could only write in his journal while sitting in his favorite chair. He would make sure he would not be interrupted by turning off his phone, having his journal and pen, bringing in a cup of coffee, and settling down to write. What David is using is the principle of association. He is actually more motivated to write because he now *associates* his chair, and even his cup of coffee with writing in his journal. By actually setting up a regular writing habit and creating an environment that supports his journal writing, David is much more likely to write on a regular basis. Certainly there are days when David probably doesn't feel much like writing at all, but having an established environment and ritual for writing will help him write regularly.

Write Regularly

Both Cari and David used the power of association and ritual to keep their journal writing practice a regular and ongoing part of their lives. Like brushing your teeth, eating well and exercising, journal habits can be made a part of your regular schedule. The value of an established routine or ritual is that it keeps you on track without having to re-establish the habit on a daily basis. Let's say for example you go to the gym three days a week at 7:00 in the morning. Some days you look forward to going, other days you feel neutral, and then there are days where you feel you just can't do it. Since your gym workout schedule is already established, you go, no matter what. You needn't debate the merits of going or whether or not you even feel like going that day. You simply dress and start your workout. Almost inevitably, you feel better. The trick is not having to re-decide each day, but to make the commitment and keep to the routine.

Create a Writing Ritual

The same is true for journal writing. Once you commit to writing a certain number of times or minutes per week, you do it. You don't have to debate about it. There will be days when you look forward to writing. There will be days when you feel neutral about writing. There will also be days where you are convinced you have nothing to say. On days like that you write anyway, even if what you write is "I have nothing to say." Explore not having anything to write about and see what emerges!

Take Your Journal on the Road

You can add variety and expand your journal writing practice by taking your journal with you to new places. Create a deeper dimension in your writing by packing your journal in your briefcase, backpack or purse for short entries during the day. Experiment with new places to use your journal. Try writing on the bus or train. Try writing at the library. Experiment with your journal sitting by yourself in a coffee house.

Quick Check

Finding the Right Time and Place to Write

❑ Are you writing at a time when your energy is high?

❑ Are you free from disturbances and interruptions?

❑ Is the setting peaceful and quiet?

❑ Is it well-lit and ventilated?

❑ Are you comfortable and relaxed in this location?

Selecting Your Journal and Pen

This book has been designed as a workbook, with the intention to read and write as you go. You can, of course, use another journal of your choice. Hopefully, when you finish this workbook you will select another journal and continue your entries.

Select Tools for Comfort

It is not likely you would start any new project without first giving consideration to the tools and equipment you will need. You wouldn't expect a carpenter to build a home without the correct tools, or a mechanic to repair your car without the right parts. Nor would you expect an artist to paint without canvas and brushes. Journal writing, too, requires some special tools of the trade.

The focus of this section is to help you decide the best tools and equipment to use for your journal. The main rule is that you write with items you feel comfortable with. If what you are using works for you and gets you writing, than you have selected the right tools. Here are some guidelines.

Be sure you feel comfortable with your selected tools.

You *Can* Judge a Journal By Its Cover

No matter what the old adage tells you, sometimes you can judge a book by its cover. The outside of the journal must appeal to you, interest you and entice you to open it. Now is a good time to consider finding a journal that's right for you. In making your selection, consider color, texture, and design.

If you are using a bound journal, the type most often found in stationery and book stores, there is an endless variety of colors and textures to choose from. Some are plain, others have a wide variety of designs or pictures. Simply choose what attracts you.

But It's Too Nice to Write In...

Many times, after explaining the importance of finding an attractive journal to motivate you, I'm met with the response, "But I'll mess up a 'nice' journal. I'm afraid to start writing in one of those nice books."

You needn't spend your life savings on a new journal. Some bound journals in many book and stationery stores, begin at $4.95. If it makes you feel better, start your new journal with an entry something like this:

> *I'm afraid of making a mistake in this fancy new journal....*

or whatever else comes up for you. I've often thought of making a large ink spot on the beginning of the first page of a journal, then realizing it was no longer perfect and moving on from there.

Sometime ago I gave a friend a beautiful bound journal as a gift. I know she thought it was lovely to look at. I also know she carefully packed it away in a drawer because it was "too pretty" to actually write in. While journals do make wonderful gifts, make sure your daily journal doesn't inhibit you from writing in it.

Finding the Right Size Journal

The size of your journal also depends on personal preference. You'll want to take into account your lifestyle and whether you will tote your journal around with you. While a standard size is 5½"x 8½", journals can be as small as 3"x 5". On the other hand, if you prefer a larger writing space and are especially likely to write in one location, you might prefer an 8½"x 11". If you clip things, save copies of letters and theater programs, or would like the space for illustrating in your journal, a large journal is essential.

A Journal By Any Other Name

You might also consider other types of books not even designed as journals. A hard cover art or sketch book can make an excellent journal if you like the freedom of unlined paper and have an interest in doing art work as part of your journal keeping practice. An accounting journal or a full page per day desk calendar might even work if you like to write on lined paper.

When selecting your journal, take your time. Roam book stores, art stores, office supply and stationery stores for ideas. Also consider making or sewing a journal for yourself. Using colors and fabric you love, you might design your own journal. Over the years, many of my workshop participants have created beautiful and elegant hand crafted journals.

When finding or creating your personal journal, there are no right or wrong choices. If, in fact, a spiral bound notebook is all you need, use that. These suggestions and guidelines are only ideas to inspire you, or get you going if you are stuck or unmotivated.

When I began journal writing in my teen years, one of my first journals was the back of my algebra notebook. Unfortunately I frequently wrote in it during algebra class, which may or may not account for why I did so poorly in math. Nonetheless, my need to write was stronger than finding the perfect place to write, or obviously, the perfect time. Don't let the selection of your journal paralyze you and keep you from writing. The only right choice is to find a journal that gets you writing, keeps you writing and allows you to get the most benefit from the writing.

Selecting Your Journal

Quick Check

- ❏ Does the outside cover of the journal appeal to you and get you to want to open it and write?
- ❏ Is your journal a convenient size for you?
- ❏ Is there adequate space for writing?
- ❏ Does the style of your journal meet your current needs?
- ❏ Does the journal you are now using or had been using still interest you?
- ❏ Is there a journal you would prefer or enjoy using more?
- ❏ What type or style of journal would work best for you right now?

Selecting the Right Pen

Pens come in many colors as does ink. Just check any good office supply, stationery, or art store. While there is nothing wrong with a pencil, for journal writing you might prefer a pen. Writing with a pencil makes the entry less permanent, and more likely to be smudged or erased.

Find a pen that feels comfortable in your hand. If you are writing a long entry, you'll appreciate a pen that feels good. Try several different types of pens and see what you like best. The color and how the pen looks will also influence your decision.

Years ago, I met **Patti** at a journal workshop. She told me that she liked the idea of journal writing, but seemed to have no motivation to write. I asked her about her pen. She told me she had been using a bright orange pen. A moment later, Patti smiled sheepishly as she explained to me she hated the color orange!

Quick Check

Selecting Your Pen

- ❏ Do you like the appearance of your pen? Is it a color and design you enjoy looking at?

- ❏ Do you like the color of the ink?

- ❏ How does the pen feel in your hand? Is it too big or too small? Does it fit comfortably?

- ❏ Does the pen move smoothly on the surface of the paper?

- ❏ How does the weight of the pen feel in your hand?

Remember, the journal is a place of record for the growth and process of your internal life. Your pen is the instrument you use to record this process. Select your journal tools and equipment with care. Be willing to let go of a notebook, journal or pen that is somehow stopping you from using your journal to its fullest. Using the back of an old algebra notebook might do the trick in terms of providing paper, but it might not do much for your creativity. (Unless, of course, you really like math).

Part II
Stops Along the Way

Chapter Three

Free Form Writing

It is time I started a new journal. Come my unseen, let us talk together.

Katherine Mansfield

If writing a perfect journal entry is what is stopping you from using a journal, you are in for very good news. The Free Form entry is designed to be written with no structure nor form whatsoever.

No structure or form means there are no rules. No rules means, you simply can't do it wrong! Incomplete sentences and thoughts are fine here. No red pen will correct your grammar or syntax. Creative spelling is invited. Free Form writing not only releases you from traditional writing blocks, it can help you become more centered and aware quickly and painlessly. In a word, it's foolproof.

Free Form Writing means no rules.

The structure-free nature of Free Form writing is what allows it to go in almost any direction and is exactly what creates so many more options. When you have fewer limits and restrictions, you have more possibilities and choices. Remember that increasing options is what allows you to more easily create change.

Nothing New Under the Sun	Certainly Free Form Writing is not a new concept. It has been used most notably in literature by James Joyce in *Ulysses* as well as the war-torn story told by Erich Remarque in *All Quiet on the Western Front*.

In literature this form of writing is known as *Stream-of-Consciousness*. Here the author takes the liberty of not following normal rules of punctuation and sentence structure. The words in this format better reflect how most of us really think, moving around from one thought to another, questioning, repeating, and exploring open-ended thoughts, phrases and feelings. We often think in spurts and fragments, not complete sentences.

In psychological terms, this form of thinking is known as *Free Association*. Sigmund Freud originally used this method in the practice of psychoanalysis. As the creator of the "Talking Cure," Freud believed that when feelings, ideas and emotions are allowed to emerge spontaneously from the unconscious, repressed traumatic experiences come into awareness.

Similar to the psychoanalytical technique described above, Free Form writing fits naturally into the context of journal writing as used throughout this book — awareness to increase self-knowledge and therefore enhancing the ability to create change. By not editing or interrupting the natural process and flow of awareness, what was unconscious can become conscious.

Free Form Writing By Another Name	In the current works on journal writing or related creative writing techniques, several others have used some form of Free Form writing. Peter Elbow in *Writing With Power* and Bruce Ballenger and Barry Lane in *Discovering the Writer Within* describe a method called *freewriting*. Essentially, they encourage the writer to keep moving the pen, to write without thinking or censoring, to allow tangents, to relax and have fun. Christina Baldwin in her book, *One to One: Self Understanding Through*

Journal Writing, calls a related technique *flow writing*. She describes a two-step approach beginning with focusing on a particular idea or thought and then allowing the writing process to increase awareness.

Natalie Goldberg in *Writing Down the Bones: Freeing the Writer Within*, calls this sort of writing a timed exercise, the basic unit of writing practice. She advocates these straightforward and clear rules: "keep your hand moving, don't cross out, don't worry about spelling, punctuation, or grammar, lose control, don't think, don't get logical, go for the jugular."

Free intuitive writing is one of the basic diary devices presented by Tristine Rainer in *The New Diary*. The method "releases the voice of the subconscious by removing or putting aside the control of the conscious mind." You relax, empty your mind and wait for whatever comes up. *Rapidwriting*, letting the words spill out without stopping to critique or correct or rearrange for the purpose of separating out the process of writing as opposed to editing, is described by Henriette Anne Klauser in *Writing on Both Sides of the Brain*.

All of these approaches essentially describe the same thing. This unstructured, formless flow of writing allows the writer to increase awareness by exploring as deeply as possible with no restrictions. The more open-ended the form, the more valuable is the tool for exploration, growth and transformation.

How Free Form Writing Works

My method, **Free Form Writing**, combines many characteristics of these related forms as well as deepens the awareness process. It is both *free* from rules and *lacking in form* and restrictions. Free Form Writing allows your inner material to freely emerge from the unconscious, unedited.

The purpose of Free Form Writing is to begin with the current level of awareness and move progressively deeper. The process itself is simply a recording on paper of the current flow of thoughts and feelings. *But it is the writing itself, combined with a slowing down and tuning in to the body and senses, as well as deepening of the breathing, that serves to increase the awareness.* In the vernacular of gestalt therapy, it is moving the focus from what is currently in the background (what is unaware) to the foreground. In workshops, I have described this method of writing as "an awareness continuum on paper." Shifting in this way can bring about increased clarity, resulting in a more focused, present, and centered feeling.

Note that in Free Form Writing, no punctuation is necessary. No attention to particular details or correct syntax nor spelling is important...only the flow of the feeling. If you imagine a swirl of paint, free flow writing gives an impression of color, line and depth without necessarily having any real direction or confining sort of outline or structure.

To create a visual image of Free Form Writing, imagine yourself with a large piece of paper, flow pen in hand, and an uninterrupted thought, every word literally connected. By unlocking the tight structure of the writing, you allow a flow of formerly unconscious awareness to surface. In doing so, you increase your awareness and make formerly unconscious feelings and thoughts available and accessible to create new options.

When to Use Free Form Writing

Use Free Form Writing anytime you feel scattered, "spacey" or out-of-focus. Remember, if you feel stuck or uncomfortable or lost in any way, write that out, as well.

Amy, a regular journal writer, shares her Free Form entry:

> *It feels good to just be sitting here, at last. I feel like I have been running in circles and not getting anywhere. I have a vague sense of uneasiness or uncomfortableness, and just feel sort of out-of-touch or something. I think I'll just become very quiet now and let myself slow down, and do some deep breathing. There, that feels better now. So what am I noticing? The birds! Wow! Were they here before? Of course they were, I didn't hear them, too spaced out. Now I hear people across the lake. Their voices rise and fall like waves of sound around me. There is a rhythm now, a rhythm as regular as my own breathing...*

To write an entry using Free Form Writing, you'll find it easy to follow these basic steps:

How to Use Free Form Writing

1. Begin by closing your eyes.

2. Breath slowly and deeply (if you are not already doing so, let your stomach inflate on the inhale, and deflate on the exhale).

3. Loosen clothing that feels tight or uncomfortable.

4. Remove shoes if you'd be more comfortable.

5. When you are feeling relaxed, begin writing.

6. Allow your writing to flow without your internal editor, judge, or critic.

7. Write without blocking or stopping yourself.

8. Write exactly what comes up for you, what you are aware of, feeling or thinking.

9. Don't worry about punctuation, grammar or syntax; allow your spelling to be creative.

10. What you are writing does not need to make sense.

11. If one thought seemingly interrupts another, simply allow that to happen; let your thoughts bounce off each other, mingle or just remain as they are.

12. Let questions remain unanswered, let thoughts be incomplete.

13. If you become stuck in this exercise, write that out. Notice what happens when you acknowledge exactly where you are.

14. Continue with this exercise for at least ten minutes, longer if you wish.

Directions

Try writing a Free Form entry below:

Stop & Write

_____

_____

_____

_____

_____

_____

_____

_____

_____

_____

_____

_____

_____

_____

Free Form Writing Revisited

Free Form Writing is a wonderful jump start method to begin your journal if you haven't written in a while or if you don't know where to begin. Its freedom, deliberate lack of definitive direction and sense of flow may put your internal critic out of a job!

Chapter Four

Beyond "Dear Diary..."

I must write it all out, at any cost. Writing is thinking.
It is more than living, for it is being conscious of living.
Anne Morrow Lindbergh

When most of us think of diaries in general, we are likely to remember quasi-leather volumes with gold-plated keys. We are likely to imagine Anne Frank's description of a "cardboard-covered notebook" where we confessed our innermost worries, fears and doubts.

Diaries in fact, have a recorded existence as far back as the Tenth Century. Although their appearance may have changed, their purpose has long remained the same—to record the existence and detail of our daily lives. While this is the most common use of the diary, it is certainly not the only one.

This chapter, "Beyond Dear Diary," addresses several other deeper uses of the daily diary method. Increasing sensory awareness, deepening the consciousness of our emotions and feelings, and becoming aware of our internal dialogue are all ways to increase the value of the Diary Log. As we increase

Use Sensory Awareness to Deepen your Diary Log

Experimenting during a journal writing workshop, **Holly** began her Diary Log with the following traditional style entry:

Wow, it actually rained today! After seven years of drought, it sure felt great!

There is of course, nothing wrong with Holly's entry. As we talked further in the workshop, however, Holly added several sensate details:

It was a rare, rainy California morning. Having lived in drought conditions for seven years, the smell of early morning rain delighted me. It teased my nostrils and played with memories from long ago. I remembered the worm hunts of my childhood, running outside in a plastic crinkly raincoat and red rubber boots just as a storm ended to count the worms in the cracks in cement, poking in the wet dirt with a discarded popsicle stick. The cleansing smell of the rain, and the years fell away. My memories shifted to inclement weather days at school, playing relay games indoors and square dancing in the gym. And the heavy snow days, propped outside my parents bedroom door with my sisters, waiting for the radio to announce school closings for the day.

While both entries discuss a rainy morning after several years of drought, look again at the second entry. In it, you can *smell* the rain, *see* the red rubber boots, *feel* the crinkly raincoat and the damp ground after a rainstorm. What's different about the second entry, is the use of the senses. The first entry reports, only. The second entry is rich and full of sensory detail.

Now you try it. Pick an event from yesterday or this morning. Begin with "just the facts." Write down only what happened.

_____

_____

_____

_____

_____

_____

Stop & Write

_____

_____

_____

_____

_____

_____

_____

Now go back to this entry. Close your eyes. See what happened. What were you wearing? What did you look like? What colors were in this picture? Were there bright or muted tones? What did you feel like? Can you identify any particular feelings? Body sensations? Aches or pains? Good feelings? Sad feelings? Check again. What did you touch? Were surfaces rough or smooth? Was it damp or cool or warm or dry? What sounds did you hear? Was there music? Nature sounds?

Go back and work with this "bare bones" entry. Be conscious of all the sensory input, the additional information you gain when you pay attention to your senses. Write down what you notice this time.

Stop & Write

_____

_____

_____

_____

_____

_____

_____

_____

_____

_____

_____

_____

_____

_____

_____

_____

_____

_____

_____

_____

_____

_____

Now read over the second version of your entry. You will probably find it a richer, more interesting, deeper entry. You have gone beyond reporting. You have touched, smelled, seen and felt your experience. Not only does this create more powerful, descriptive and alive reading for you to review, it also trains you to more keenly observe things around you. It helps you to attend to details at a more conscious level and to fully experience day-to-day events.

Become Conscious of Your Feelings

In addition to increasing and enlivening your sensory awareness, you may also use the Diary Log to deepen your consciousness of emotions and feelings. Insights and understanding of needs, formerly below conscious level, now become available. Decisions such as major career changes, endings of relationships, choices that can change the course of your life, become known. Even less significant awarenesses can have impact in what Fritz Perls, founder of gestalt therapy called, "Aha" moments. Aha's are when we "get it," the flash of insight like the turning on of a cartoon figure's light bulb. What was unknown becomes known so clearly, we wonder why we hadn't seen it all along.

This entry illustrates how the recording of emotions and feelings brings them into greater consciousness and awareness.

> *Maybe I should just call this entry Confessions of a Substitute Teacher. Early this morning I was thinking I've actually trained myself to wake up and read the clock out of only one eye. Every weekday morning, it's Russian roulette, never knowing, never knowing. My friends can't get a straight answer, "Do you work, or don't you? I don't get it."*

> *I don't get it, either—although sometimes I do, depending on who needs a sub. A "sub," now that's an interesting word to be applied to a person with five years of college education and a Specialization in Elementary Teaching. A sub what? Submarine? A boat, submarine? A sandwich? Sub. Sub. Sub-standard? I certainly hope not.*

Sitting in immaculate piles on my dining room table, categorically arranged are the best children's books the public library has to offer. Little popsicle sticks huddle together, to eventually form puppets for some lucky class. Little games, gimmicks, anything educationally sound, to grab the kids and bring them under my power.

It's hard, a damn hard job to do. Each day is a new experience. You never know what grade, what district, for what teacher. And you never get the long term rewards. But there is something else, a sense of inner freedom, a sense of being present, of completing one day at a time. Yet chances are, I will never see these kids again. The teacher and I, like silent partners, phantom ghosts, left only to guess at each other's ages and vital statistics.

I grumble, I mumble, I complain. And yet, sometimes, I like it. I liked it, even this morning, still shower-damp, and spilling hot coffee down my sleeve on the way to my car. I liked it, even a sixth grade. Three minutes before class the principal walked in, sort of in a chatty way, "Ah, this is a rough class."

I swallow. Why me? Why am I doing this? I know in my heart and soul I am doing the best I can. It just never seems enough. There is so much anger here, so much lashing out, so little respect for each other, and more frightening, so little respect for themselves. I feel so torn, it's only a job, it will be over soon. And yet I feel sad. Is this what I do best? Is this where I need to be?

I am tired beyond belief. There must be a way I can give, but I must remain whole to be able to give at all...

In the previous entry, the awareness was both a surprise and a relief. The writer was surprised at the depth of her love for teaching and at the same moment relieved to find her career had unknowingly shifted emphasis, opening new possibilities for her creativity. When she allowed her feelings and inner thoughts out, she could see them more clearly. Her increased awareness allowed her more options, even to the point of a new career path.

Begin a new Diary Log entry now. Use the same topic you used before, or if you like, choose a new one. Write about a recent event in your life. As you write, pay attention to your feelings and to your emotional responses. Write beyond what happened, beyond the "he said, she said" component; write about the feelings that accompanied the situation or about the feelings you now have as you focus on the event.

_____

_____

_____

_____

_____

Stop & Write

_____

_____

_____

_____

_____

_____

_____

Write with a conscious-ness of your feeling state.

Now re-read this entry. What do you notice about it? Does the entry intrigue you in any way? Is it interesting? Does what you have written remind you of anything else? As you respond to questions about your own experience, you are deepening your emotional or feeling consciousness. As you become more consciously aware of your feelings, your journal, and, most certainly your life, becomes richer, fuller and more alive.

Record Your Internal Conversation

We have discussed using the Diary Log to first deepen sensate awareness. Secondly, we used the Diary Log to deepen the awareness of emotions and feelings. A third way to use the Diary Log is the recording of our internal conversation. A friend of mine says she has such a continually rich dialogue in her head, that she sometimes puts her fingers on her lips to see if they are moving. You can begin to use the Diary Log as a place to record the inner thoughts, conversations, running commentary, and editorial remarks that are an ongoing part of your day-to-day "talk to yourself" process.

Seth, a client of mine, shared the following entry with me:

> *If I have to sit here one more minute and listen to this garbage, I think I'll puke. We've gone over and over this and not one person can seem to get to the point. Hold on, the new guy is talking. Great, he just used the words "personal responsibility" 15 times in three minutes. Maybe he could take a little personal respon-sibility and come up with an original thought.. I'm going to lose it.. I can't go on. Maybe I could kind of sneak out and go to the john. Sort of forget to come back.. Wait.. Mr. Responsibility is winding down. What is it about him that's driving me nuts? Gees, he reminds me of my dad, lots of hot air. Do I do that? Lots of air, no substance???*

By being aware of both the positive and negative feedback you tell yourself, you can observe your own self-talk. As you in-crease your awareness you begin to sort out those messages that you want to keep and those you want to delete. Perhaps you give yourself messages that are previous recordings of someone else's opinions and ideas. Maybe what you tell yourself is a message and belief from long ago and no longer applies to who you are today, in this moment. As you become aware of what works and what no longer works for you, you have more options, and more of an opportunity to change.

Record the conversation you're having inside your head.

The Diary Log is perfect for moving your deepest thoughts and feelings from the hidden private stage of your mind to the "public" stage of a blank piece of paper. While diary recordings should never be designed for public viewing, the movement from the most private hiding place of the mind to a piece of paper can provide you with powerful insights.

Try writing a new entry now. Start by focusing on some recent event. It might be a discussion or a conversation you had with someone else. Summarize the conversation or the event. Now write down whatever else you were thinking or feeling at the time, the parallel or internal conversation. Don't edit. Keep writing. Put down all the fantasies, "should haves," nasty little thoughts, opinions, judgments, all those things you would normally edit out. Keep writing. Notice how you are feeling as you write. Keep going and keep that editor at bay. Begin your entry here:

_____

_____

_____

_____

_____

_____

_____

_____

_____

Stop & Write

There is tremendous freedom in this type of entry. It allows you to stay tuned to your own process without interruption or interpretation by someone else. It allows you to look at your own experience through a private magnifying glass, looking closely at yourself in relationship to the event. From this perspective of your increased awareness, you have opened up the possibility of many more options. By considering and taking ownership of all that you said and felt, you now can look at the situation again. What if you had said this? Should you have said that? If you could do it again, what would you do differently? How else could you have handled that? What did you learn about yourself from this situation that you were unaware of before?

Quick Check

Creating Diary Log Entries

❏ Are you using sensory details in your entry?

❏ Are you fully exploring colors, tones, sizes, shapes and other visual clues?

❏ Are you using auditory information such as nature sounds, music, voices around you, or even the sound of silence?

❏ Are you using kinesthetic or physical sensations? Are you aware of how your body feels or felt if you are reporting an event? Are you aware of the air, the textures, the smells, the feel of the surfaces you're touching and the ground you're walking on?

❏ Are you noticing the feelings that surface as you write? Are you staying with the feelings that come up for you, even though they may feel painful, uncomfortable, or even just new and different?

❏ Are you listening for the conversation in your head that is going on even as you record this entry? Are you noticing the judgments, the inner dialogue, the fears, worries and concerns? Are you noticing the private joys and pleasures you experience as you write?

❏ Are you paying attention to what you learned from what you just wrote?

Using your senses to develop awareness, getting more in touch with your feelings, and tracking your inner monologue is what gives the Diary Log its richness and depth. These new tools can take you far beyond the traditional "Dear Diary!"

Using these three tools, write a final diary log entry. (If you're stuck, sneak a look at Chapter 12 for ideas to jump start your entry.)

Stop & Write

_____

_____

_____

_____

_____

_____

_____

_____

_____

_____

_____

_____

_____

_____

_____

_____

_____

_____

_____

_____

_____

_____

_____

_____

_____

_____

_____

_____

_____

_____

_____

_____

_____

_____

_____

_____

_____

_____

_____

_____

Chapter Five

Maps of the Mind

The mind's cross-indexing puts the best librarian to shame. *Sharon Begley*

Since maps are essential to travel, it seems appropriate to be discussing mind maps as we move forward on our journey. While the editing process so essential to writing is primarily a left brain process, the creative idea formulation stage of writing is a right brain process. Together, the collaboration between both sides of the brain can create depth and richness in your journal entries.

Mind maps, branching or clustering, as they are sometimes called, allow us more access to our creative side. The mind map, a simple skeletal drawing, helps us create ideas in a non-linear, non-logical fashion.

The Value of Mind Maps

For some people it is easier to see and understand information if it is set out and formatted in a more free form style. While lists, lines and boxes clarify for some people, others may respond better to the use of mind maps. Mind maps are more open-ended, and allow for a holistic or Big Picture orientation. You can use a mind map to problem-solve, plan or organize. The following mind map, for example, illustrates the contents of this book:

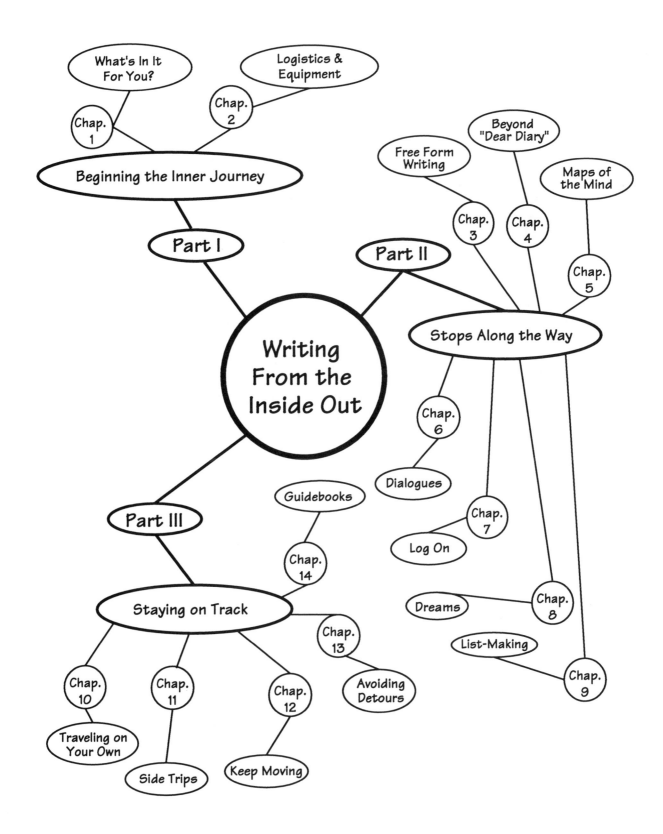

Using a Mind Map to Problem Solve

In my practice, I work with many individuals on life planning and the development of personal goals. Mind maps work well for this purpose.

Bridget, a woman in her early fifties, knew she wanted to create her own catering company. She had worked for many years for several larger companies and was now ready to move off on her own. As I talked with Bridget, we wrote down both the key points of her past accomplishments and her future goals. She listed her culinary and design skills and her skill with people, her organization skills and her ability to envision a final event in detail. Bridget found it easier to see her skills when she viewed them in the following format:

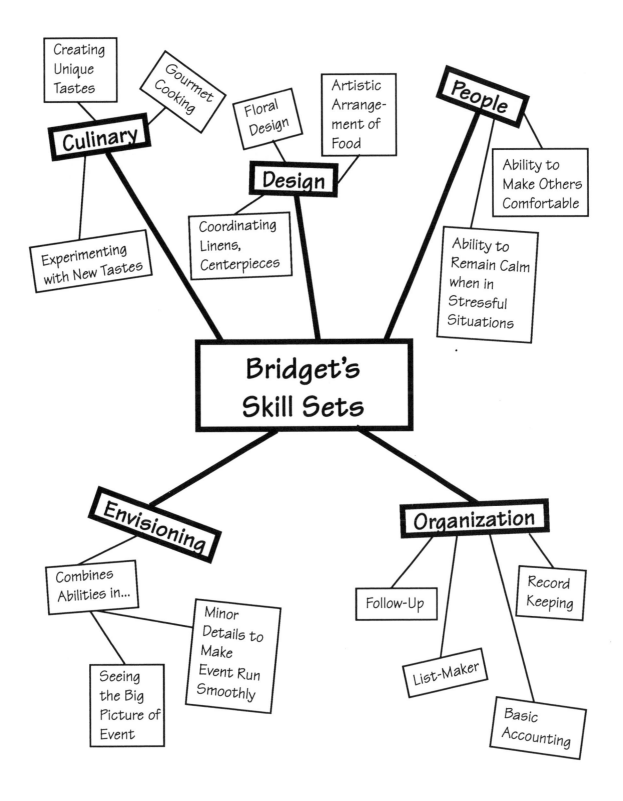

Creating Unique Tastes

Gourmet Cooking

Culinary

Floral Design

Artistic Arrangement of Food

People

Ability to Make Others Comfortable

Design

Experimenting with New Tastes

Coordinating Linens, Centerpieces

Ability to Remain Calm when in Stressful Situations

Bridget's Skill Sets

Envisioning

Organization

Combines Abilities in...

Minor Details to Make Event Run Smoothly

Follow-Up

Record Keeping

Seeing the Big Picture of Event

List-Maker

Basic Accounting

Niklas, a man in his 30's came to see me about re-focusing both his personal and professional goals. We began with Niklas creating a mind map of his working values and "wanna be" values. A portion of Niklas' mind map is shown:

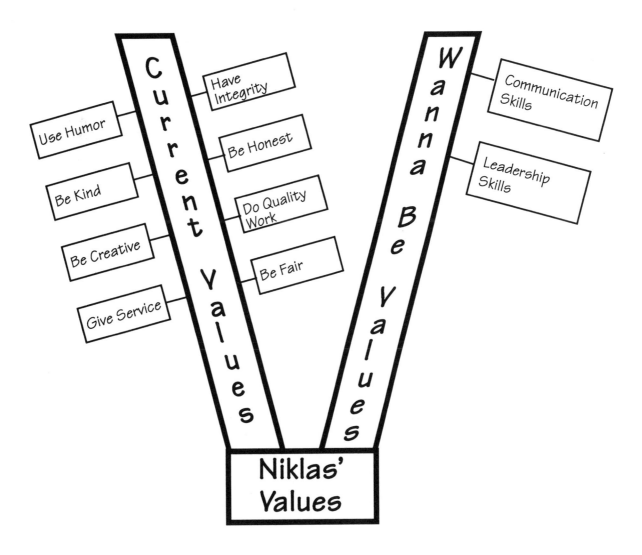

Using his values or principles as a guide, Niklas next created a rough long-range mind map for his goals:

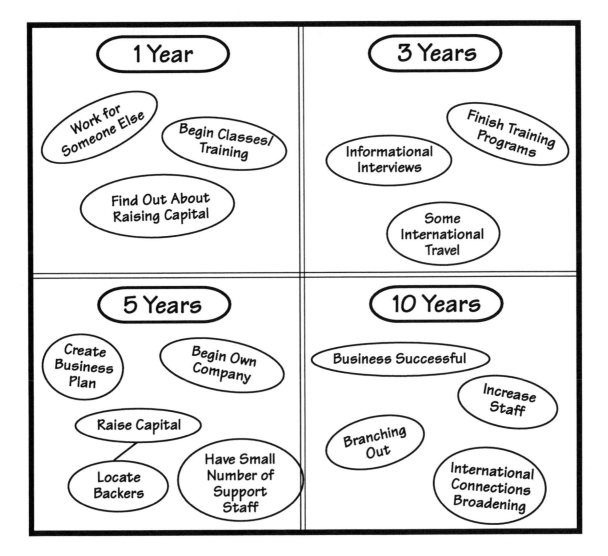

In a few sessions, Niklas had clarified both his principles and goals. Next, Niklas looked at those issues that prevented him from accomplishing his goals. Another mind map provided the following help:

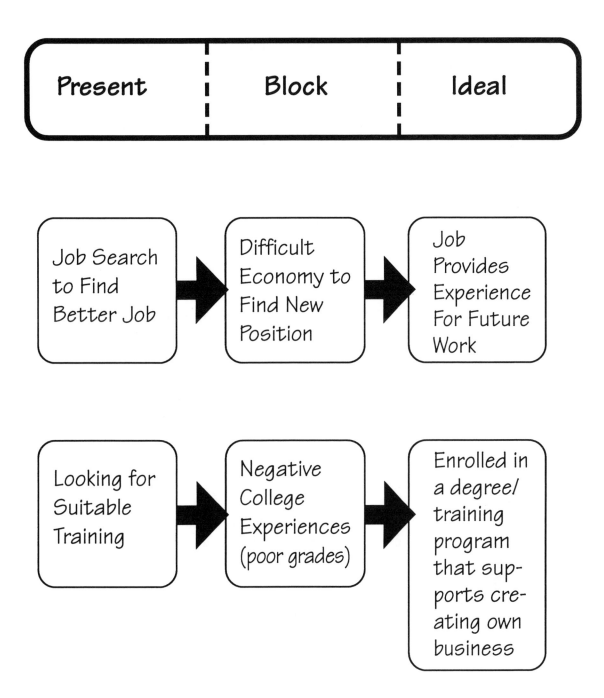

A mind map is different from a chart, graph or linear way of problem-solving. A mind map will not *solve* your problem. It will, however, bring you some clarity and a different perspective. By creating a holistic vision of the problem, you are more likely to create a viable solution and explore options you might otherwise have missed.

How to Create a Mind Map

Directions

Perhaps you have a stuck place or challenging area in your life that could be clarified through the use of a mind map. Here are some easy-to-follow guidelines to get you started:

1. Become quiet. Allow the chatter inside your head to be still.

2. Let your breathing slow and your body relax.

3. Allow your mind to be open and your thoughts and feelings to flow freely.

4. Let a picture of a problem area or challenge in your life, surface.

5. Make a circle, box or other drawing and write in it the central question or problem.

6. As you think of associated questions, solutions, or ideas, write them down. Use lines to show relationships between items.

7. Use crayons, colors, pictures in any way that helps to clarify.

Stop & Write

You are now ready to complete a mind map on your own on the next page. Begin by filling in the center circle with the topic, problem or challenge you wish to work with. Fill in the other circles as well.

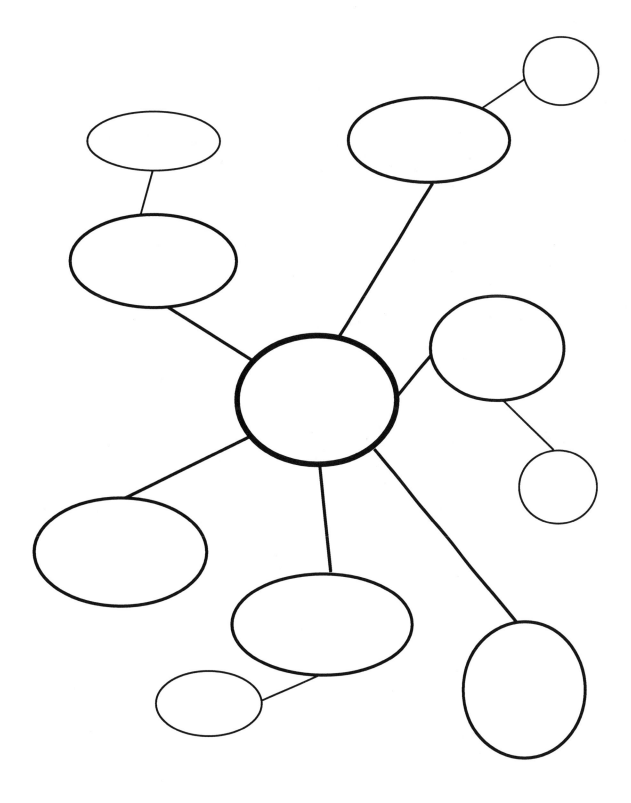

Here is another mind map pattern to try:

Create a mind map of your choice, here:

**Stop &
Write**

Using a Mind Map to Organize

As with using a mind map to problem solve, mind maps also work to organize because of their holistic or Big Picture orientation. Because a mind map views a situation from the large perspective, you are less likely to leave out main steps or important details. To plan a dinner party, to re-model, to pack, to plan a vacation, or simply to make a grocery list, a mind map is an organizing tool. Here are some examples:

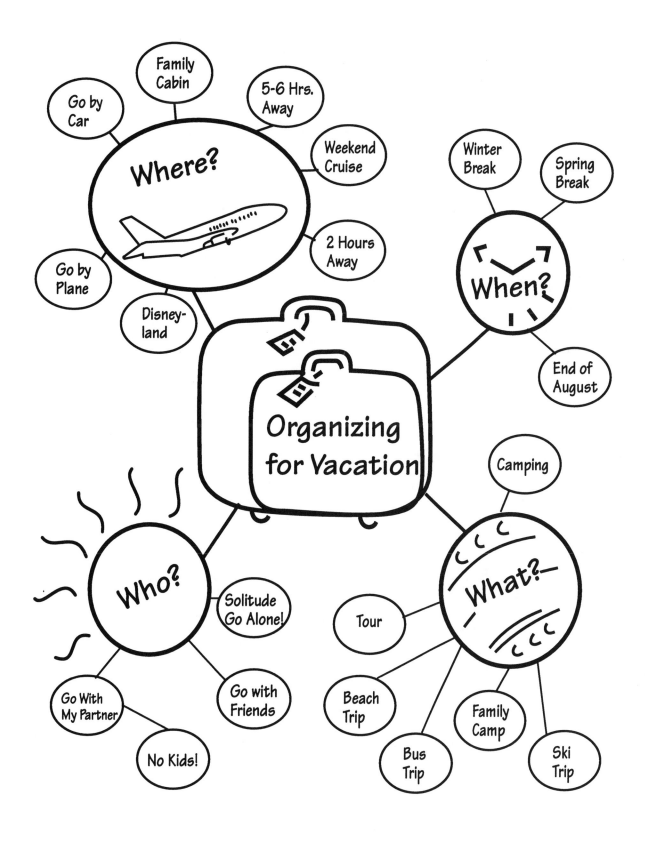

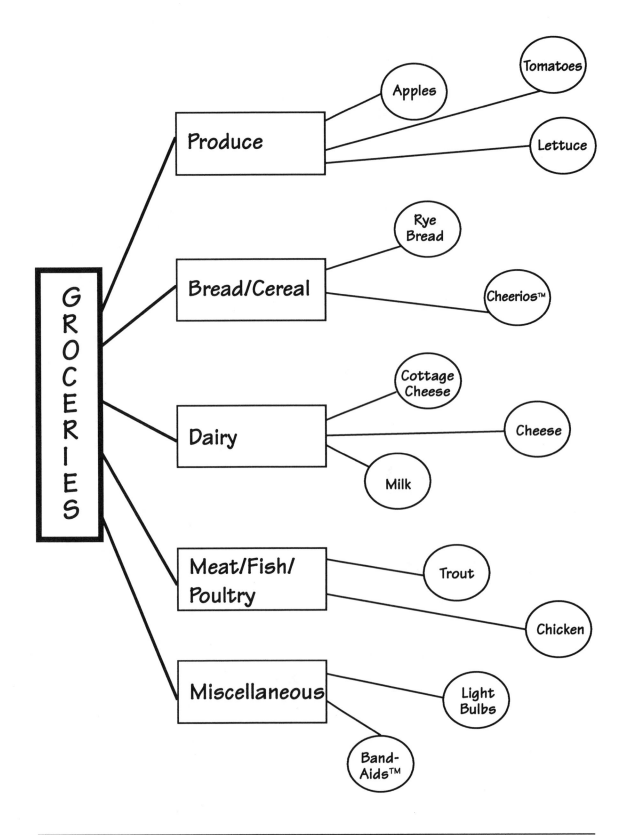

Create a mind map to organize a project or priorities for yourself. Remember, there is certainly no right or wrong way to create a mind map. Let yourself explore all possibilities!

Stop &
Write

**Using a
Mind Map
to Plan**

In addition to using a mind map to organize and problem solve, you can also use a mind map to plan. **Maria** already knew what was involved in planning a Recognition Dinner for her agency. She had focused on the purpose, solved many of the logistic and on-site problems and done almost all of the tasks involved to create a smoothly running event. To make sure she hadn't forgotten any important components of the dinner, Maria created the following mind map as a final planning tool:

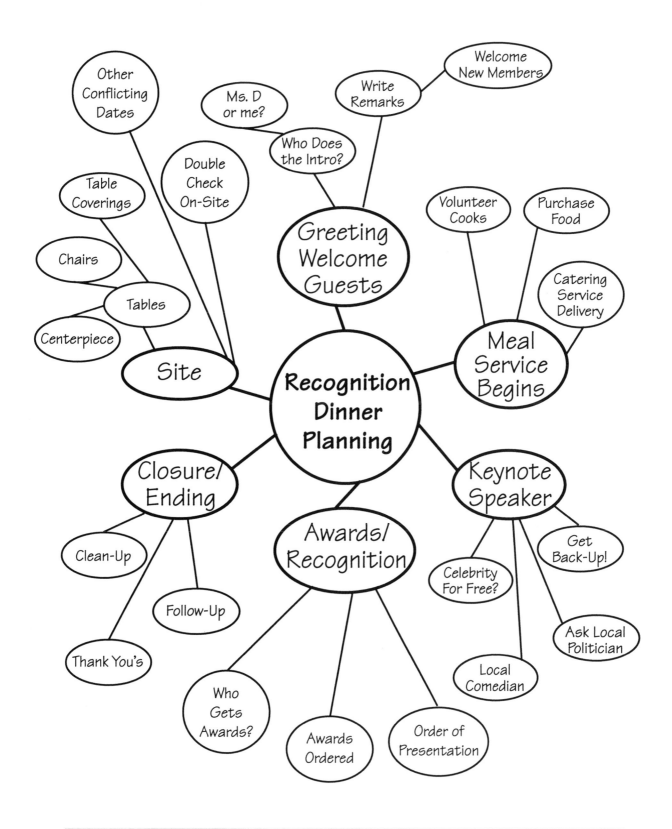

Stop & Write

Experiment with a mind map in which you are planning an activity or event. Use any shapes, forms or designs that support your creativity!

Create your own planning mind map here:

Remember, these exercises are designed to be exploratory and creative. Don't rush through them. Take your time and enjoy!

Chapter Six

Dialogues...Writing From Your Inner Voice

Who sees the other half of Self, sees Truth.
Anne Cameron

Although each type of entry presented in this book offers some type of deepening awareness, the dialogue is one of the most powerful. The dialogue is a method joining conflicted or alienated parts of the self or the self in relationship to other people or entities. The dialogue helps us to complete the unfinished business of our lives, to bring together what is separated, to heal what is broken.

How the Dialogue Works

Over twenty years ago, as a gestalt therapist in training, I discovered the dialogue method quite by accident. I found that by combining a basic gestalt therapy technique referred to as "two chair" dialogue and my own love of the journal as a method to clarify and release feelings, I had created a powerful tool for self-therapy.

Many years after my own discovery, I found others had also developed similar methods. If you enjoy the use of the dialogue in your journal, Ira Progoff's work in Depth Psychology, *At a Journal Workshop,* and Piero Ferrucci's *What We May Be* are excellent resources.

Constructed very much like a dialogue in a play, the written dialogue places conflict into an open arena for discussion rather than maintain its usual position as an endless circular argument in our heads. By writing the dialogue out on paper, we release it from the private corners of our minds to more conscious awareness on paper.

Dialogue With Yourself

Conflicted Roles Dialogue

The easiest way to begin to describe the types of dialogues is to begin with the dialogue with the self. How many times have you caught yourself debating, discussing, even arguing with yourself about conflicted duties and roles?

Jeff was torn between a vacation with his wife and son and visiting a seriously ill favorite uncle who lived on the other side of the country. His obligation to his family was tearing him apart. He had diligently planned, prepared and saved for his long overdue, upcoming vacation to a resort, where it was difficult to get reservations. In addition to his own personal disappointment and need for a vacation, Jeff was worried his family would feel both deserted and angry if he changed the vacation plans. On the other hand, the uncle had been a role model for him when Jeff was a young man. They had been very close and Jeff anguished over his uncle's declining health. He decided to dialogue with the two internal, conflicting roles.

Jeff began by identifying his conflicted roles. He realized he was struggling with his role as father and husband and with his role as nephew. Both were important, both needed to be honored and heard:

Husband & Father: *Oh, boy. I'm really in trouble now! I can't disappoint Jason and Patty. They were really counting on this trip.*

The Good Nephew: *I know they're counting on the trip—and so were you. I'm really stuck here because Uncle John is really sick. I just feel like I need to be in two places at once.*

H & F: *That's exactly the problem, I do need to be in two places at once. I feel strongly about being with my wife and son, they don't get to see me enough as it is. But I'm really worried about Uncle John. He's my family, too!*

TGN: *I have a thought. Let's look at the actual travel arrangements. When do you have to be at the resort?*

H & F: *Well, we were going to leave here on Saturday morning on the train so Jason could see parts of the country he had never been to. We planned to arrive on Sunday afternoon to be ready for the activities on Monday morning.*

TGN: *You'd have to miss the train ride there, but you could leave Friday morning, visit with Uncle John over the weekend and fly out to meet Patty and Jason by Sunday night.*

H &F: *Wow! Great idea. It's lots of traveling, but I could do both that way.*

TGN: *It's not a perfect solution and it's certainly more expensive, but it just might work....*

Jeff now was able to clearly express both sides of his conflict, and to clarify and finish each thought. As he listened to himself in his dialogue, Jeff realized he had resolved his dilemma. His increased awareness of his thoughts and concerns created options. Options now provide him with creative choices.

Do you have conflicts in your life? Are there roles and obligations that seem to be battling inside of you? Stop for a moment and generate a list of those current or unresolved conflicts between roles in your life.

Stop & Write

1. _____

2. _____

3. _____

4. _____

5. _____

Conflicted Aspects of Your Personality

Jackie's conflict was between roles she played *inside* of herself. Jackie raised four children and had, in many ways, been a traditional, "Perfect and Always Available Mom." She carpooled her children to sports practices and games, baked cookies for the school bake sales, and participated as an active member of her church. Jackie was a surrogate mom to her children's friends. When her children left home, Jackie felt a sense of loss. She had never taken the time to explore her strong interest in art, although she had used her artistic skill in creating beautiful artistic surroundings in her home. Jackie wanted to study, and to travel and see the original paintings of the masters. In fact, Jackie's long held fantasy was to paint. Her dialogue went like this:

Perfect Mom: *Well, this must be what they mean by the Empty Nest Syndrome. I feel like I should be happy the kids are doing so well, but I just feel kind of down in the dumps and out of sorts. I don't know what it is. I just feel at lose ends.*

Wanderlust Artist: *It's funny. When you were so busy over those years, you used to think about me. I was your escape—what you would do if you ever got the time.*

PM: *Now, time is certainly not the issue. I've got plenty of that! I'm just not sure what I want to do with it.*

WA: *Why don't you ask me what I would like to do with it?*

PM: *OK, since you want me to ask, I'll ask. What do you think I should do with the time I have now?*

WA: *I want to go back to your fantasy. What did you always want to do when you had the time?*

PM: *Oh, come now! That's silly. I'm too old for that sort of thing. I'm just too far along in my life to think about art now!*

WA: *I'm not suggesting you become a world class artist.*

PM: *What, then?*

WA: *I think you can still explore your interest and obvious artistic talent.*

PM: *What do you mean?*

WA: *You can start with something as basic as an art class at the rec center or a junior college.*

PM: *OK. Then what?*

WA: *That will get you started painting. You can also look into travel courses with an emphasis on painting and art.*

PM: *Hmm....*

WA: *What do you think?*

PM: *It feels a little scarey at this stage of the game, I mean I'll probably be the oldest one in the class or on the tour.*

WA: *Hardly! Besides, you bring maturity and experience...*

Look at your own life for a moment. Do you ever feel like Jackie, conflicted between various parts of your own personality? Perhaps there is a part of you that is highly responsible and another part of you that longs to break out of your day-to-day routine. Maybe there are parts you have kept hidden for so long you have forgotten they even have a voice! Try making a list of your own inner sub-personalities here:

Stop & Write

1. _____

2. _____

3. _____

4. _____

5. _____

To create a dialogue with yourself, simply follow these basic guidelines:

How to Create a Dialogue with Yourself

1. Select either two roles you play, or two sub-personalities that are in conflict.

2. Give both parts in your dialogue a working title. Titles can be shortened or given nicknames as you continue to write.

3. Decide who will begin "speaking" first.

4. In beginning any entry, allow yourself to become quiet, let your breathing slow and deepen.

Directions

5. Take a few moments to become comfortable and quiet within yourself.

6. When you are ready, begin writing your dialogue.

7. If one part of your dialogue becomes stuck, write that out as part of the dialogue.

8. Continue writing your dialogue until you feel the parts shift their point of view or reach some sort of resolution.

Begin your dialogue here:

Stop & Write

_____

_____

_____

_____

_____

_____

_____

_____

_____

_____

_____

_____

_____

_____

_____

_____

Dialogues With Others

You now have the basic format for creating dialogues. There are many types of dialogues you can now create. A very useful dialogue is the dialogue with others. This type of dialogue is useful in dealing with unfinished business, dress rehearsals of conversations you would like to have, or simply clarifying issues you may have with someone else in your life.

Kim felt estranged from her mother. In public they were courteous and polite to one another, but Kim never felt her mother truly understood or acknowledged her. Kim's mother recently died and although Kim missed her, she needed to say things to her mother that had never been said when she was alive. Kim had the following dialogue with her mother:

Kim: *It never occurred to me I could talk to you like this. I mean it feels weird, especially since you're dead.*

Kim's Mother: *Well, the fact is, we didn't talk all that much when I was alive. Why not do it now?*

K: *I don't know what to say to you. In fact that was always the problem, I never knew what to say to you.*

M: *I know exactly what you mean. I never knew what to say to you either.*

K: *You're my mother, what do you mean you didn't know what to say to me!*

M: *I always wanted to be close to you. I used to cry because it always felt like my only daughter hated me. You always seemed so critical of everything I did. I had no idea how to talk to you.*

K: *I was critical of you! That's a good one! You were totally judgmental of me. The boys were perfect and I didn't fit your image of what a good daughter was supposed to do.*

M: *What was a good daughter supposed to do? What was a good mother supposed to do? The boys weren't perfect by any means. They were just easier, not so moody, more easy going.*

K: *See, there you go again, with your judgments. Why couldn't you just accept me as I was, moods and all?*

M: *I did accept you. I loved you with all my heart. I just never knew how to express it.*

K: *Oh, right, was I just supposed to read your mind?*

M: *(Silence)*

K: *Well, say something! You never said you loved me, how was I supposed to know?*

M: *I don't have the answer to that. When my mother died I was so young, I hardly remember her. My father never talked about his feelings, never expressed anything loving to us.*

K: *I know your mother died when you were little. How come you didn't talk to me about it? How come you never told me how hard your life was for you?*

M: *That's not how we did things, not in my family, anyway. If you were in pain, it was private, you kept it to yourself.*

K: *It sounds like you kept the pain inside, and meanwhile you couldn't express joy, either.*

M. *I guess not. The thing that makes me sad now is how much I hurt you. I really did love you. I loved to watch you play when you were a little girl. I loved to listen to you when you sang your little songs and danced. Sometimes I would come in while you were sleeping at night, just to watch you sleep.*

K: *You told me that, that you watched me when I was sleeping, but I never believed you.*

M: *Why not?*

K: *It just seemed odd to me, it was so touching, in a way, but it didn't fit for how I knew you.*

M: *It seems like we both felt we didn't know the other.*

K: *I wish I had talked to you a long time ago.*

M: *I wish with all my heart we had this talk, too.*

Perhaps one of the most healing elements of the dialogue is to make the unknown known. Then solutions and resolutions can begin, as your new options become clear.

Do you have people in your life with whom you would like to talk? Are there conversations you have fantasized? Remember, whether a person is alive or not, or whether or not you are still actively in a relationship with him or her, you may still have something to say. Begin a list here of those people you would like to dialogue with:

Stop & Write

1. _____

2. _____

3. _____

4. _____

5. _____

To create a dialogue with others, simply follow these basic guidelines:

How to Create a Dialogue with Others

Directions

1. Select a person with whom you have unfinished business. (This could be anything at all that feels unsaid or incomplete.) It can be a current relationship or a relationship from the past.

2. Give yourself and the person you are talking to a working title. Titles can be shortened or given nicknames as you continue to write.

3. Decide who will begin "speaking" first.

4. As in beginning any entry, allow yourself to become quiet, let your breathing slow and deepen.

5. Take a few moments to become comfortable and quiet within yourself.

6. When you are ready, begin writing out your dialogue.

7. If one part of your dialogue becomes stuck, write that out as part of the dialogue.

8. Continue writing your dialogue until you feel the parts shift their point of view or reach some sort of resolution.

Begin your dialogue on the next page:

Stop & Write

_____

_____

_____

_____

_____

_____

_____

_____

_____

_____

_____

_____

_____

_____

_____

_____

_____

_____

_____

_____

_____

_____

_____

_____

Other Types of Dialogues

You can essentially create a dialogue in any area of your life where you experience conflict or alienation. Dialogues create a unique opportunity to resolve unfinished business. If you are stuck, dialogue with your job or even the furniture in your living room.

The following section is designed to generate ideas for creating your own dialogues:

If you are struggling either in your career choice or your day-to-day work routine, set up a dialogue with your work. If your career feels like it's in a rut or you're bored at even the thought of going to work, ask your working life what it would like to be doing.

Professional or Working Life

Your body can provide you with a rich dialogue if you listen. Ask your body the meaning of a symptom pattern, ache or pain. Talk with your body about addictive behavior or compulsive eating. Ask a binge what it needs from you.

Body

Do you have a physical space that is not exactly as you'd like it to be? Do you have a room that needs to be re-decorated and you have no idea where to begin? Start by asking your space or room how it wants to reform itself.

Environment

Would you like input from great-great grandparents? Are there religious or political figures you wish you had known and whose advice would inspire you? Talk with them.

People in History

Remember those moments when you made a decision that had a major impact on you or some aspect of your life—to leave home, to move, to be with a particular partner, to have a child, to change careers. Go back to that crossroad, finish the piece you have never managed to complete.

Moments in Time

Dialogue with a theme that seems to follow through in many different aspects of your life. The theme may be a feeling such as anger or depression. It may be a characteristic or quality in your life such as a sense of chaos or chronic lateness.

An Ever Present Theme

Spiritual Self/ Inner Guide/ Higher Self

When we are centered with ourselves, we can recognize that part of us that is wise. Create a dialogue with your own source of inner wisdom. Then become quiet enough to listen.

Guidelines for Other Dialogues

The guidelines for all other types of dialogues are similar to the guidelines for Dialogues with Others and Dialogues With the Self. Think in terms of possibilities when it comes to creating dialogue. Design your own unique dialogues. Be creative.

Directions

1. You can create a dialogue between any two or more conflicted or alienated parts, roles, feelings or entities.

2. Your dialogue is like spoken dialogue, there can be interruptions, incomplete thoughts and sentences.

3. If you are unsure how to begin, imagine each of the parts or players in your script have their own voice. Have the voices converse with one another.

4. When you begin any entry, allow yourself to become quiet, let your breathing slow and deepen.

5. Decide who will begin "speaking" first.

6. Let your dialogue flow instead of forcing an outcome.

7. Give yourself and your dialogue partner a working title. Titles can be shortened or given nicknames as you continue to write.

8. If one part of your dialogue becomes stuck, have that voice talk about being stuck.

9. Continue writing your dialogue until you feel the parts shift their point of view or reach some sort of resolution.

Deepening the Dialogue Process

If you would like to go even further with the dialogue, you can deepen the process. When exploring relationships with others, especially historical figures or individuals, you may want to pretend you are a newspaper reporter. Gather facts and data before you begin your dialogue. Research information about your dialogue partner.

You might also want to sit quietly or meditate about the person or entity in your dialogue before you begin writing. Let yourself imagine visiting the person. Close your eyes. Visualize the person you are visiting sitting next to you. Notice how they look. What are they wearing? What are they doing? What sort of expression do they have on their face? Now notice how you feel in your own body. What sort of physical sensations and feelings are you having? Pretend you have started the dialogue already. What does your voice sound like? What does the other person sound like? Begin your dialogue with these voices.

If you become stuck in the writing of your dialogue, say so. As in a spoken dialogue or conversation, sometimes the process of simply stating the obvious breaks the deadlock.

If you should come to a total standstill during your dialogue, and you have no idea how to proceed, it might be time to take a break. In our lives, we frequently are unable to complete conversations. Yet when we have an opportunity to finish what we were saying, ideas often seem clearer when we return to them. The same is true for a written dialogue.

As you become comfortable and familiar with the dialogue process, you will find yourself solving problems that seemed impossible to solve. You will automatically create new solutions by creating new options.

Create Your Own Dialogue Index

To review and for your future reference, compose a list of people and topics with whom you want to dialogue at a later time. (You will probably discover you'll have many additions to this list as you complete the workbook.)

Dialogues With Conflicted Roles (see list you started on page 68)

Stop & Write

_____ _____

_____ _____

_____ _____

_____ _____

Dialogues With Conflicted Aspects of Your Personality
(see list you started on page 70)

_____ _____

_____ _____

_____ _____

_____ _____

Dialogues With Others (see list you started on page 74)

_____ _____

_____ _____

_____ _____

_____ _____

Other Types of Dialogues
Working Life, Body, Environment, People in History, Moments in Time,
Ever Present Theme, Spiritual Self

_____ _____

_____ _____

_____ _____

_____ _____

Chapter Seven

Log On...Narrative and Record-Keeping Logs

The journal is a record of experience and growth, not a preserve of things well done or said.
                                        Henry David Thoreau

Logs are a perfect place to track the everyday details of a project, process or experience. The journal is a place to house your logs. Logs can be designed in anyway you like. The strength of the log comes in consistent recording. By writing even a brief entry on a regular basis, you will see steady, on-going progress over a period of time. By reviewing your daily entries, you may discover your progress and growth is quite remarkable.

I have several clients with issues regarding their weight. One such typical client, **Marci**, decided to go on a diet. She had never had much of a weight issue, but as she matured, she found her body's metabolism seemed to slow down. In the past, she could change her eating habits for a few days and easily drop a few pounds.

One day, Marci realized she was rapidly gaining weight and her old solution no longer worked. She researched and found a healthy weight reduction program. As she began her new program, Marci made notes about her progress. She wrote several times a week, noting not just the changes on the scale, but how she felt about herself as she was losing weight. Marci also noted the food she was eating and the exercise she was doing throughout the week. As her weight loss continued, Marci began to notice patterns in her eating. She noticed, for example, she had a tendency to overeat when she was angry or upset. She also frequently binged when she felt the need for personal space.

What Marci created was a combination of a record-keeping and narrative log. The record-keeping portion of her log contained her actual weight on a week-to-week basis. In addition, she kept a food log, where she wrote down what she ate, when she ate it and the quantities of food eaten. Marci's log also contained her exercise program, listing the type of activity, the intensity of the workout and the length of the workout. This portion of the log was objective data, recording actual numbers and facts.

Marci also created a section in her log for subjective data, writing down her observations and feelings about her weight loss. Her log contained patterns, observed highs, lows and plateaus. Using both subjective and objective data, Marci's log became an invaluable support tool. Here's a portion of her narrative log:

Day 1: *Super motivated this time! I'm really going to do it!*

Day 4: *Still feeling really good. A little sore from my morning walking, but I enjoy it.*

Day 7: *Really challenging weekend! I actually turned down a piece of chocolate cake, and got by with only a bite. Now that's a first for me!*

Day 12: *I haven't written in a few days, felt like I was too weak to hold the pen. I'm losing weight, but I'm starving to death. I'm so sick of eating carrots!*

Day 16: *This is making me crazy! The kids brought home Halloween treats— this just isn't fair.*

Day 21:   *Three weeks. Actually I'm not doing too badly. I notice that as I lose weight, exercise more and eat less and different foods, I have more energy. Also notice drinking water seems to help fill me up.*

Day 28:   *Rough weekend again, food-wise. I notice when I'm stressed or tense, food calms me. I've got to find other ways to calm and soothe myself.*

Marci combined the benefits of a record-keeping log (pounds, weight, food eaten) and a narrative log like the one shown above. In fact, Marci's situation is not unique. A recent study shows that on-going use of a written log may as much as *double* weight loss results.

What supported Marci in her weight loss was recognizing her progress. If she had no feedback or no place to observe her progress, she might have made unwise food choices. Marci stayed on track by increasing her awareness. She had more options because she had more information. With more information, she had the ability to make better choices.

Vince, a well educated technician, kept a log for a different purpose. He had recently lost his job and was about to begin a full-scale job search. He knew his choices went beyond just getting a new job, but would influence his career direction and life-style for the future. Fortunately, Vince had resources to cover him for several months in his search. He reasoned that time well-spent in the data-gathering and planning stage would directly influence the outcome of his search.

Vince decided he would keep a log with two separate sections. The first part was a record-keeping log. He wrote down how he spent his time each day, with whom he spoke or interviewed and a brief summary of any points he had researched. Although many days felt unproductive, he continued with his log, depending on it to keep track of his activities and his next steps.

In the second component of his log, Vince recorded his observations and feelings about his progress, the responses and feedback from interviews, and the research he was doing. Well into his job search, Vince re-read his entire two-part log. He realized that the job he was attempting to find was no longer what he really wanted to do. In the course of recording both his daily activities and his feelings, thoughts and responses, Vince realized an interest he always had in starting his own business. In addition to his technical skills, he was a focused, self-starter with good "people skills." He realized that instead of trying to find a job working for someone else, he would be better off working for himself and creating a market for the skills he had.

Vince did start his own business and has become a successful entrepreneur in the process. Although his business is still small, he has tremendous potential to create both growth and additional earning capacity.

To discover the value of using an ongoing log for yourself, consider some of these uses:

- Progress on a remodeling or construction job (include costs, contacts, feelings about the remodeling as it proceeds).

- Progress in taking a class or learning a new skill (particularly useful to measure progress if the skill or subject area you are learning is challenging).

- Progress with a child with a learning disability or school related problems (include changes in parenting styles, meetings with school counselors and teachers).

- Progress in purchasing a new home or an extensive search for a new location (for added value, keep detailed notes of contacts, costs, and specific locations and features).

- Progress in a stepfamily (observing interaction between family members and changes in feelings).

- Progress in personal therapy, noting patterns, new awarenesses, changes from old patterns of behavior.

- Progress in a fitness or workout program, noting activities, increased endurance and outcome.

Now, take a look at your life. Is there a project, interest or goal that could be assisted by regular logging of data or feedback? List possibilities here:

1. _____

2. _____

3. _____

4. _____

Stop & Write

The value of using a log as a personal growth and change tool is to recognize your progress. The magic of the log is the steady day-to-day rhythm that develops in ongoing or frequent recording. A half-pound weight loss or a single interview may be a minor accomplishment. Yet they are steps forward to true growth and change.

Here is a summary of the steps to create either a narrative or record-keeping log:

How to Create a Log

Directions

1. Begin by closing your eyes.

2. Breathe slowly and deeply; let your stomach inflate on the inhale, and deflate on the exhale.

3. Imagine what you would like your log to be able to do for you on its completion (i.e. contain a record of the progress of your weight loss, contain details of your job search).

4. While remaining quiet and uninterrupted, ask yourself what type of log would best serve your needs. What components, categories or characteristics does your log need to contain?

5. As you begin your first entry, note the date, time and place of your writing. Note this information each time you add an entry.

6. Remember, the more regular and frequently you write, the more the log can measure your progress.

7. The value of the log appears greater after a period of time has elapsed.

As you've read this chapter and noted ideas for your own logs, perhaps you would like to begin a log entry now. Later, you can transfer this log to another journal if you would like.

Stop & Write

_____

_____

_____

_____

_____

_____

_____

_____

_____

_____

_____

_____

_____

_____

_____

_____

As discussed in the summary of steps for creating a log, remember that a log is a type of entry that provides growth and satisfaction over a long period of time. Begin a log, continue it with regularity and watch your progress!

Chapter Eight

Dreams...An Inside Job

*I believe that our dreams transport us through the
underside of our days, and that if we wish to become
acquainted with the dark side of what we are, the
signposts are there, waiting for us to translate them.*
                                    Gail Godwin

There is, of course, an abundance of material written on the
topic of dreams. The seemingly surreal world of our dream
state has mystified us since the beginning of our existence. Our
dream exploration will be limited here to the discussion of
dreams as they support personal growth and transformation
on our own inner journey. Included will be logistics of recording dreams and suggestions for getting the most out of the
dreams you do record.

Where Dreams Come From

Although you may frequently awake from a dream with no
awareness of what the dream means or its significance to you,
dreams are deeply connected to your inner world. Dreams form
a bridge between what is unconscious and what is conscious.

Imagine standing on the shore and looking out at the ocean. What is visible to your eye, all that is on or above the surface of the water, represents your available consciousness. All that is below the surface of the water, all that lives, swims and is alive below the level you can see, represents your unconscious or subconscious. Just because you can't see it does not mean it doesn't exist. A whole kingdom of life exists below what is visible to your eye.

Recording Your Dreams

Imagine the recording of your dreams like a huge fishing net. At first, you will pull in all kinds of things that may not be of value. Like fish that are too small, and pieces of debris that you don't want or need, there may be little value in what you first catch. But as you increase your frequency at casting your net, and your skill at fishing improves, you will catch bigger and more valuable fish. To improve the value of your "catch," this section provides some suggestions for recording your dreams.

It May Take A Few Tries

Over the years I have spoken to many clients who say, "But I don't dream, what am I supposed to do?" I gently suggest that while it is possible that they don't dream, it is not likely. What is more likely is that they do not *remember* their dreams. Try some of the suggestions below. I'm sure your dream recall will improve.

Set Yourself Up Before You Go to Sleep

Even before you go to sleep, you can help yourself remember your dreams. Right before sleeping, say an affirmation like, "I will remember my dreams with ease." Programming your unconscious for several nights will give you much clearer dream recall.

Have a special dream notebook, journal or tablet and working pen placed next to your bed.

Here's a client's story. One morning, **Judy** woke up very early with an especially rich and colorful dream. As she had just learned about recording dreams, Judy was particularly excited about writing down her dream. She wrote quickly, noting all the details she could recall. After a few minutes of recording, Judy was satisfied she had written down all the rich details, and felt the dream was particularly full. She drifted back to sleep for a few more hours, smiling to herself as she anticipated working with her dream later on in the morning.

Unfortunately, when Judy looked at her journal to begin working with her dream, all she saw was a few words in faded ink and the rest of her dream etched into the paper where her pen went dry! Judy had been half asleep when she wrote her dream, not noticing her pen was out of ink!

One of the best ways to use your dreams is to ask a specific question before you go to sleep. Let's say you are having a problem at work, or in a personal relationship or even about the general direction to pursue in an important decision in your life. Try asking yourself a question you would like answered, before you go to sleep. You've heard the expression, "sleep on it." Ask yourself a question and then, sleep on it.

Ask Specific Questions For Your Dreams to Answer

Bonnie had been struggling with whether or not to take a promotion at work. She debated the pros and cons. If she took the promotion, her income, status and career potential would be enhanced. However, she would also be spending less time with her family, more hours at the office, and increasing her level of stress. Bonnie asked the question: "What choice will be the happiest and healthiest regarding my work?"

Another key point in the recording of your dreams is to write quickly without stopping as soon as you are awake. Half awake will also work. Try to write before you get up and move around or go to the bathroom. Thirty percent of our dream recall is lost just by getting up and moving around. Once you are awake and relatively conscious, you might even try to re-create the position you were in before you woke up. This will help extend the sense of still being with the dream.

Write Quickly, Before You Move Around

Use a Tape Recorder If It's Easier

If tape recording is easier than writing, leave a small tape recorder next to your bed. You can dictate into your tape recorder without distracting yourself or disturbing your dream recall. Remember to allow time later in the day to listen to the tape.

Write Down Your Feelings

In addition to noting your dreams, write down the feelings you have in the dream. If the dream has left you particularly elated, or depressed, lonely, sad, anxious or joyful, write that down, too. Your feeling states will be an important part of understanding your dreams, later.

Learning From Your Dreams

You may have dreams that appear to be about things that are happening currently in your life, about specific people and situations. They may represent fears and anxieties you have repressed or ignored. Recording the dreams can help with solutions to problems or may provide a new perspective.

A friend of mine told me she dreamed for several nights of losing her driver's license and then her wallet. I asked her what her wallet and its contents meant to her. She told me her wallet represented her identity. She also told me that although she liked the new man she was seeing and was attracted to him, he had a very strong presence and sometimes she felt he overwhelmed her. A few minutes later, she stopped mid-sentence as she described the feeling of losing her own identity to him. She grinned as she realized she had just used the exact same words in describing the lost wallet in her dream!

Watch For Metaphors and Humor

Over the years I have noticed that dreams with important messages for me are frequently located on college campuses. Dreams with profoundly important messages for me often unfold at an ivy league school. I especially enjoy the subtlety of this metaphor. My dreams clearly advise me that an important message, a pay-attention-and-learn-from-this-dream-message, is available by literally putting me in a school setting!

Your dream life can also have a sense of humor. Several years ago, I remember waking myself up laughing in the middle of the night. Earlier in the evening I recall feeling hurt by a thoughtless remark made at a dinner party. Instead of becoming angry or depressed, my unconscious chose to create inappropriate lyrics for a popular song. I woke to a familiar tune with lyrics that had me giggling. My unconscious dream process created a delightful alternative to heal my hurt feelings.

Watch For Patterns and Themes

When you have been recording your dreams and working with dream material for some time, you will probably begin to notice a series of reoccurring patterns and themes. Pay attention to them. The fact that they do reoccur means they are likely to have an important message for you. You may also notice that particular characters continue to re-appear. Pay attention to these characters as they create your own personal dream language, your own private dictionary.

Kelly shared her dreams on a regular basis and continued to dream of a childhood acquaintance. The child in her dreams always threatened Kelly in some way, either physically or emotionally, leaving her feeling vulnerable and insecure. As we explored what this dream figure might represent, she realized that her dream acquaintance was a part of her self who felt threatened and insecure. Kelly also realized that this particular dream figure came to her on a regular basis when she was especially challenged at her work. Her dream acquaintance was simply the projection of a part of her personality.

The Prophetic Dream

Sherry Ruth Anderson, in her book, *The Feminine Face of God,* writes that the concept of her book emerged from a powerful prophetic dream. She states her openness to not understand its meaning at the time was what allowed her to learn from the dream for many years to come.

Just because you don't understand a dream *at the time,* does not mean it is not significant. Perhaps you are not ready or able to understand its full meaning. Simply record your dreams as they occur. Your journal of dreams may prove valuable and prophetic when re-read at a later time.

Not All Dreams Move You Toward Growth

Not every dream is deeply significant. It may enhance something you already know. You may find yourself awakening with a sense of clarity or certainty. Something you had been debating for a long time may suddenly become clear to you, as if you had known the answer all along.

As you are learning about dreams, write down each and every dream as you remember it. Later, you may find that not all dreams are worth recording. Some images are a clearing of the day's events (like watching the news or a scarey movie before going to bed.) For now, however, assume there is usefulness in every dream. Record the dream, then decide later if you want to work with it.

Before we go further in working with dream specifics, take a moment and record a recent or powerful dream. If you are not in the habit of recalling your dreams, return to this section as you become more aware of your dreams.

Record a recent or especially vivid dream here:

_____

_____

_____

_____

_____

_____

_____

_____

_____

_____

_____

_____

Stop & Write

Dream Specifics:
How to Work With a Dream Image

Now that you have recorded your dreams, we'll explore specifically what to do with a dream image.

Give the most significant individual or object in your dream a voice. It's OK if this seems strange at first. Speak from the first person singular voice. Remember, all parts of the dream are a projection of you. That means each "voice" is a part of you that you may or may not be aware of. The purpose of dream work is to discover and integrate all of your parts.

Give the Most Powerful Parts of Your Dream a Voice

Remember Bonnie from the earlier example, trying to make a decision about a promotion at work? She asked the question, "What choice will be the happiest and healthiest regarding my work?" Let's see how she created a dialogue from her dream to help find a solution.

> *I am walking through a jungle with thick underbrush. Everywhere I turn, the sunlight is blocked by the denseness of the jungle. Eventually I come to a clearing with a waterfall. It is a beautiful shimmering stream of water, sparkling like diamonds as the sun hits its surface. To reach the waterfall, I must cross over a huge pool of water. The water is so deep I can't see the bottom. I begin to swim across but realize I will never make it so return to the shore. How will I ever get to the waterfall? An exotic bird catches my eye. He is perched on a tree. As I move toward him, he flies off, but leaves a branch hanging. I climb the tree. From no where a rope swings downward. I realize the rope had been hidden by the branch. It isn't a strong rope, risky to swing from, but it may get me to the other side.*

Bonnie identified the following parts in her dream:

1. Herself

2. Thick jungle brush

3. Waterfall

4. Deep pool of water

5. Exotic bird

6. Rope

Create a Dialogue Among the Parts in Conflict

You already know how to create a written dialogue. Now create a dialogue between any two or more parts that seem to be in conflict or struggling in some way. The parts represent a conflict within you that you may or may not be aware of. Write out the dialogue and continue to a resolution.

In our example, Bonnie identified the jungle underbrush and the waterfall as the two most divergent parts of her dream. She chose to facilitate the dialogue by entering it herself. She created this dialogue:

Bonnie: *I'm not sure why I chose you both, but you seem the most significant to me. Listen jungle, why are you so difficult and hard to get through?*

Jungle: *Because I'm your life! I am complex, it's true, but sometimes you just experience me as a thick, difficult struggle.*

Bonnie: *But my life is complex! I have a lot of demands on my time and energy.*

Jungle: *That's what the waterfall is about.*

Bonnie: *What do you mean?*

Jungle: *Why don't you ask the waterfall?*

Bonnie: *OK. Waterfall, what are you doing here?*

Waterfall: *I flow freely, falling as I may, no restrictions, just enjoying the sun and the ride down stream...*

Bonnie: *But how can you help me?*

Waterfall: *Maybe you could be a bit more like me, let go a little, just enjoy the ride for once.*

Bonnie: *That's easy for you to say! You obviously don't have a demanding job, two children and a husband! How am I supposed to be like you? Besides, how do I get over to your side anyway, the water is too deep and far.*

Waterfall: *A little bird let you know there is a rope swing. Maybe you could use that.*

If you find that your dream is not providing you with meaning, it may simply need time to incubate or settle. Continue to work with it anyway. Sometimes, after several days or even several hours, the significance of the dream will become clear to you.

Dreams May Need Time to Incubate

Bonnie sat with her dream for a day or two. After awhile the impact of her dream figures became clear to her. Bonnie, in fact, could move more easily between the thick, crowded demanding part of her life and the more free flow life she longed for. Soon after her dream, Bonnie created a job share plan that enabled her to continue her professional growth as well as spending more quality time with her family.

Putting It All Together

The techniques of dream interpretation presented in this chapter will give you a sense of mastery over your dreams. Although you can enlist the help of a therapist, you may be the best qualified person to interpret your own dreams.

Guidelines for Recording and Interpreting Dreams

Directions

To review the steps in recording and interpreting dreams, you might want to use the following list:

1. It may take a few tries, but stay with the process of dream recording.

2. Set yourself up to record and remember dreams before you go to sleep.

3. Ask specific questions for your dreams to answer.

4. Write quickly, before you get up and move around.

5. Use a tape recorder if it's easier.

6. Write down both your dream and the feeling state of the dream.

7. Some dreams will be about the current day-to-day problems or challenges in your life.

8. Some dreams may be prophetic.

9. Some dreams will simply confirm and verify what you already know.

10. Your dreams may contain metaphors or symbols.

11. Your dreams may seem to have a sense of humor about them.

12. In interpreting your own dreams, take a part, person or object that is most interesting or holds the most energy for you. Give it a voice, present tense, first person singular.

13. Remember that parts of your dream are parts of you that you may be unaware of or alienated from. Working with these parts together integrates unfinished and stuck places in your life.

By recording dream patterns and themes, you will begin to understand the meaning of your own dreams.

Reoccurring Patterns

_____

_____

_____

_____

_____

_____

Stop & Write

Reoccurring Themes

_____

_____

_____

_____

_____

_____

_____

Reoccurring Images

_____

_____

_____

_____

_____

_____

_____

This chapter has invited you to open your eyes to the richness of your own dreams. They can give you an ongoing reservoir of meaning and an understanding of unfamiliar aspects of yourself. Your dreams can offer you a rich perspective of new ideas and points of view. Perhaps you will enjoy your dream state so much, you will enjoy being asleep more than being awake!

Pleasant dreams!

Chapter Nine

List-Making...
A New Twist on an Old List

Making a list and checking it twice...
S. Claus

The concept of making a list is certainly not a new idea. People have been making "to do" lists to organize and focus tasks forever. Certainly if you find list-making to be a useful tool, keep doing it. This chapter however, will introduce several additional lists you may never have thought to use. In addition, it will introduce a method that will give you a continuous flow of journal writing ideas.

The "To Do" List – Expanded

First, let's begin with the most basic kind of list. Even the word "list" generally conjures up the good old standard "to do" list. But let's add a new twist. Beyond your "to do" list for today, add to it all of the unfinished projects and "to do" tasks of your life. Go ahead, list everything, both big and small. List every nagging unfinished little project. List things you can't wait to do (probably these won't appear on your list because you've already done them!) and all of the things you've been avoiding. Stop reading, start writing.

Stop & Write

1. _____

2. _____

3. _____

4. _____

5. _____

6. _____

7. _____

8. _____

9. _____

10. _____

11. _____

12. _____

You might want to transfer your list to a separate page (or pages) at this point, but hopefully you have gotten a start. If you want to, continue with your list now, or else commit to coming back to it later.

Whether you work on your list now, or continue it in the next day or so, keep it open and continue the list for a couple of days. Make sure you write down every "to do" imaginable.

Since you have now increased your awareness to include all of the "to do's" of your life, you have several options. Here are some ways to proceed.

1. Pull out all those easy things you may be able to handle right away. Jot down the run to the dry cleaner, the quart of milk to buy at the grocery store and the five minute phone calls you need to make. Put these in your Daytimer™, daybook or calendar for today.

_____

_____

_____

_____

_____

_____

Stop & Write

2. Next, cross out those things you know you'll never do. Ever. You might know you'll never write to your Aunt Evelyn, so cross it off your list. You'll probably never finish that afghan you started seven years ago and lost the instructions for finishing. Cross it off the list.

3. Now here comes the really creative part. Look at what's left. As you skim your list, do you see patterns that are emerging? Are there things that group together automatically? Are things beginning to fall into broad headings? Perhaps you have a series of phone calls you need to make. Maybe there is an absolutely necessary bill paying and correspondence list. Maybe there are a number of house projects that need to be attended to. Perhaps there are drawers that need to be cleaned and reorganized, closets that need to be purged. Look at what items form a natural project. Group things by type or activity. Re-write

your lists by projects or groupings. If it's easier, create a mind map to organize yourself.

Stop & Write

_____

_____

_____

_____

_____

_____

_____

_____

_____

4. You may now want to look at what you learned from this master organization list. Here are some questions to get you started:

a. What type of activities are you most likely to avoid?

_____

_____

_____

_____

_____

b. Why?

_____
_____
_____
_____
_____
_____

Stop & Write

c. What do you get from procrastinating?

_____
_____
_____
_____
_____
_____

d. Do you associate unpleasant consequences with following through?

_____
_____
_____
_____
_____

e. Are there consequences from not following through?

Stop & Write

_____

_____

_____

_____

_____

_____

f. Are there real issues in your life that need to be looked at before you can get to some of your projects?

_____

_____

_____

_____

_____

_____

g. What things would never appear on your list? (Either because you have already done them, or never intend to do them.)

_____

_____

_____

_____

_____

_____

h. Why?

_____

_____

_____

_____

_____

_____

Stop & Write

Review what you have just completed. You now have an organized project list instead of an overwhelming list of seemingly unrelated "to do's." Perhaps you also have some insight into your organizational patterns, how you focus yourself, and how you avoid focusing and procrastinate. In addition, you have probably generated several expository entries or perhaps even some dialogues to help you discover more about yourself. Imagine, all of this evolved from your willingness to create a "To Do" list!

List-Making From a Kernel Sentence

Creating a list from a kernel sentence is another way to use a list as an awareness tool. To begin a kernel sentence list, you need only write two or three lead words and let the sentence complete itself. Here are some examples:

I want...

I don't want...

I resent...

I appreciate...

I'm afraid of (fearful about)...

I'd love to...

I forgive myself for...

Although these sentences don't look like much in an abbreviated form, they are powerful kernels to stimulate thinking and feeling.

Years ago in a workshop I was teaching, the whole class was delighted as a young woman begin to giggle in the middle of the "I Want" list exercise. Apparently, prior to writing her list, she had no inkling of her desire to drive a race car!

Allowing yourself to write what you really want, without editing, has a kind of magical draw. You may surprise yourself. Begin an "I Want" list, now:

Stop & Write

1. I want _____

2. I want _____

3. I want _____

4. I want _____

5. I want _____

6. I want _____

7. I want _____

8. I want _____

9. I want _____

10. I want _____

Now try some of the other kernel sentences:

1. I don't want _____

2. I don't want _____

3. I don't want _____

4. I appreciate _____

5. I appreciate _____

6. I appreciate _____

7. I'm afraid of (or fearful about) _____

8. I'm afraid of (or fearful about) _____

9. I'm afraid of (or fearful about) _____

10. I forgive myself for _____

11. I forgive myself for _____

12. I forgive myself for _____

Perhaps these lists have generated some interest for you. Feel free to expand your thoughts or feelings into another entry here:

_____

_____

_____

_____

_____

_____

_____   **Stop &**
Write

_____

_____

_____

_____

_____

_____

List-Making From Any Topic

To create a list from any topic, pick a topic, any topic, and create a series of questions to generate a new list. Why generate questions? Because generating questions causes us to automatically search for an answer. When we search for an answer we are deepening our awareness.

In a journal workshop I challenged the group to name a topic that could not be expanded. One of the words they came up with was "television." We ended up with the following list of writing possibilities to explore.

1. What was the most important thing you ever watched on television?

2. How did viewing this program influence or affect you?

3. What impact did/does television have on how you view your own family?

4. If television had never been invented, how would you spend the time you now spend viewing? How would it impact your life?

I worked with **Dean** using this exercise. He picked the topic "clocks" and generated the following list of questions:

1. What do I like or dislike about clocks?

2. What memories do I have of clocks?

3. What do clocks mean in my life?

Then Dean chose to expand the word clock to something closely related to clocks. He added the following questions:

4. Why is time such an issue in my life?

5. Why do I let my life be ruled by other people's personal time clocks?

6. Why is my personal clock always moving so fast?

7. Why do I always feel like there isn't enough time?

These two examples are random topics. Imagine what you could do with words you select!

Take a minute now and select several words. They may be random words. They may be areas of interest to you. Make a quick list of some words to work with now:

1. _____

2. _____

3. _____

4. _____

5. _____

Stop & Write

Now select a word from your list:_____

Generate as many questions as you can think of from this word:

1. _____

2. _____

3. _____

4. _____

5. _____

Finally, on the next page, write an entry answering one or more of the previous questions. Choose the questions that hold the most interest for you.

Stop & Write

_____

_____

_____

_____

_____

_____

_____

_____

_____

_____

_____

_____

_____

_____

_____

Clearly, list-making can go beyond your shopping or daily "to do" list. Using only a kernel sentence or even one word can result in an endless number of journal writing possibilities!

Part III

Staying on Track

Chapter Ten

Traveling on Your Own: Beginning the Journey

Whatever you can do or dream you can, begin it.
Boldness has genius, power, and magic in it. Begin it
now!

Johann von Goethe

You are now at an especially exciting time in your journey, since you now know the options available to you. This chapter will help you to begin your personal discovery by selecting a journal, learning how to decide which type of entry will serve your needs, and exploring an even greater number of options and possibilities.

Selecting Your Journal

In chapter 2, "Logistics and Equipment," we discussed the value of selecting a journal that is comfortable and easy for you to use. Remember, if the journal itself does not motivate you to write, you will be defeating your purpose.

Beyond color, design and the outside appearance of your journal, you will also want to base your choice on the interior and organizational style of the journal.

The most common type of journal is bound, which is by far the easiest type of journal to use. Your entries simply follow one after another in chronological order. The advantages are obvious. It is easy to use and requires no forethought or preparation. When you are finished with a particular bound journal, you have a bound volume of your life.

The bound journal has some drawbacks, however. Because entries are written chronologically, you will need to read through several pages to look for a particular entry. It is difficult to find patterns to learn from when you have to re-read the entire book to find out what you've written. Since entries are recorded in chronological order, they are not necessarily recorded in any other type of order. Dreams are scattered throughout the journal in addition to logs, free form entries and dialogues.

If you do plan to use your journal for re-reading later, you can of course mark various entries with colored ink, annotating your journal yourself. You can also attach or glue on tabs to highlight entries.

You might want to consider a loose-leaf format. Advantages of a loose-leaf journal are that related entries (dreams, logs, etc.) can be stored together. Once completed, pages can be taken out and stored both by type of entry and chronological order for easy retrieval. Your journal can also be reused many times. Through the use of an index in the front of the journal and referenced notes at the end of each entry you can track your own progress and movement through your journal.

Remember, you can change your journal at any time. Start with what seems best now.

Write a journal entry based on what you have learned so far. As you write, pay particular attention to areas of excitement and high energy as well as resistance.

Stop & Write

_____
_____
_____
_____
_____
_____
_____
_____
_____
_____
_____
_____
_____
_____
_____
_____
_____
_____
_____
_____
_____
_____
_____
_____
_____
_____
_____

Where to Go Next

The more experience you have with your journal, the more comfortable you will become in choosing the appropriate type of entry. The following summary of entry types and the entry type check list can help you determine what type of entry you would like to write.

Free Form Writing

This method of writing is the best place to start if you know you want to write, but are confused, unclear, or unmotivated. Its formlessness makes it an ideal place to simply begin writing. Begin by closing your eyes, becoming quiet and listening. Pay attention to your breathing, feel the sensations in your body, and listen to the thoughts in your head. Allow yourself to write with no purpose or goal in mind. Your ultimate aim is to clarify and center yourself.

Diary Log

This form of writing comes the closest to what we know and think of as the old-fashioned diary. It is the recording of the day-to-day events of your life. This type of entry enriches your daily experience by exploring the world with more awareness of the senses, emotions and feelings. The Diary Log also increases your awareness by calling attention to the on-going internal dialogue continually playing inside your head.

Mind Maps

The mind map balances the linear, logical left side of the brain with the holistic, creative right side. Integrating the use of mind maps in the daily journal creates more powerful insights by truly writing with both sides of the brain.

Dialogues

This is perhaps one of the richest types of entries. Its richness lies in the number of options available. The basic method is to literally create a written dialogue between conflicted or alienated parts of your self. The dialogue is also used to resolve conflicts with others and unfinished business in any area of your life.

This section emphasizes the benefits of on-going logs and record keeping. Included are logs for health, weight loss, exercise, projects, and completion of tasks. The purpose of the log is to measure progress and growth by written tracking on a regular basis.

Narrative and Record-Keeping Logs

Recording dreams as entries over a period of time can be an invaluable aid in problem-solving and dealing with resolutions to inner conflict. Journal writing integrates naturally with dream work and provides an added dimension by bringing unconscious material into awareness through regular recording of dreams.

Dreams

The well-respected list gets a new twist in this version of list-making. Beyond your grocery list and daily "to do" list, this method explores the psychological list. Lists can begin with a repeated kernel sentence or be organized around a particular topic.

List-Making

Choosing Which Road to Take

You now have many options available to you. How do you decide which type of entry to begin with at any given time? The guidelines on the next page can help you move along on your journey with as few bumps as possible.

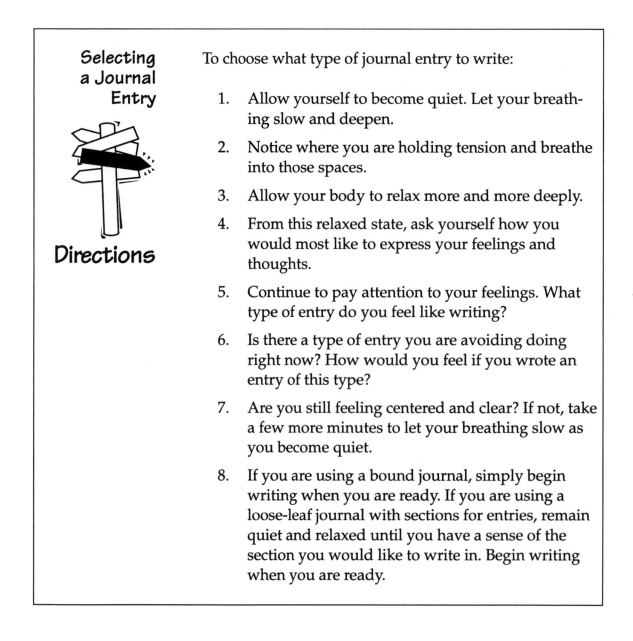

Selecting a Journal Entry

Directions

To choose what type of journal entry to write:

1. Allow yourself to become quiet. Let your breathing slow and deepen.

2. Notice where you are holding tension and breathe into those spaces.

3. Allow your body to relax more and more deeply.

4. From this relaxed state, ask yourself how you would most like to express your feelings and thoughts.

5. Continue to pay attention to your feelings. What type of entry do you feel like writing?

6. Is there a type of entry you are avoiding doing right now? How would you feel if you wrote an entry of this type?

7. Are you still feeling centered and clear? If not, take a few more minutes to let your breathing slow as you become quiet.

8. If you are using a bound journal, simply begin writing when you are ready. If you are using a loose-leaf journal with sections for entries, remain quiet and relaxed until you have a sense of the section you would like to write in. Begin writing when you are ready.

Getting Stuck at the Crossroads

In spite of a clear understanding of journal entries and the choices open to you, there may still be times when you don't know what you want to write. At these times, you might want to begin with Free Form Writing since it lacks structure. Begin your entry by describing what you feel and what you notice around you.

Vicki, a workshop participant, shared the following Free Flow entry with me:

> *Where to begin? I have no idea! I have no clue what I'm thinking or feeling. I just feel kind of numb and out-of-touch, like I'm incredibly boring or something. Maybe I'll just sit here and see how boring I can be. No! Too boring! Let's see what else. OK. I'll try to relax and breathe deeply. Wow, I just realized I had been holding my breath. And my back kind of hurts a little bit. I generally feel kind of stiff and uncomfortable. What am I holding in my back that makes it so stiff?*

Vicki then moved to a dialogue with her back in the dialogue section of her journal. The dialogue began like this:

> *Vicki:*   *I had the impression you wanted to talk to me.*
>
> *V.'s Back:*   *Thank you for talking with me, I've been trying to get your attention for some time, actually. I'm sorry I had to cause you pain.*
>
> *V:*   *Well, obviously you've gotten my attention! What is it you want me to know?*
>
> *Back:*   *These things aren't that easy for me to admit, but I'm feeling like I'm carrying a lot of old junk back here.*
>
> *V:*   *Like what?*
>
> *Back:*   *A lot of old stuff. A lot of anger and old beliefs that are keeping me rigid and stiff. I want to let go of some of this stuff and be done with it!*
>
> *V:*   *I agree with you there.*

Vicki continued her dialogue with her back until she reached a greater awareness of where her pain was coming from and how she was holding old stuck ideas and beliefs in her body.

Ron had a different experience of where to begin writing one morning. Because his dream had been especially powerful, Ron began by recording it.

> *Fragments flying around me, like pieces of a comet or some kind of colorful chunks of rock... Feel as though the pieces are all connected in some way, but they continue to swirl around my head...*

Ron knew that the "pieces" and "chunks" flying around were significant to him and clearly represented something else. He sat quietly, closed his eyes and allowed an image to present itself to him. It occurred to Ron that the dream fragments were in fact about the career and relationship choices he was currently struggling with. Like the comet pieces or rocks, each of Ron's choices had substance but did not yet fit together in a recognizable pattern.

Next, Ron chose to create a mind map, drawing out each of the qualities represented by the comet pieces/career/relationship options. His mind map looked like the one on the next page:

Ron used both the dream recording and subsequent mind map to create several dialogues with himself and others in his life. In doing so, he became clearer on the next steps on his career/relationship path.

For both Vicki and Ron the choice and direction of their entries was clear to them. Remember, however, there is simply no right or wrong choice in any aspect of keeping your personal journal. If an entry does not move smoothly or seem to fit, try something else.

In the next chapter, we will explore additional options for other types of journal entries. These additional entries can greatly enrich your journal experience. Besides, what fun is a journey without a few side trips?

Chapter Eleven

Side Trips: Quick Stops You Won't Want to Miss

Certainly, travel is more than the seeing of sights; it is a change that goes on, deep and permanent, in the ideas of living.

Miriam Beard

These additional types of entries are all designed to increase the depth and quality of your journal writing experience. They are, in fact, side trips on your journey you won't want to miss.

Each additional entry in this chapter contains a description and guidelines for integrating it into your journal. The entries will work well with both bound and loose-leaf journals. To use these entries with a loose-leaf journal, simply add a new section. If you are using a bound journal, these entries can be integrated anywhere in the journal.

Affirmations and Visualizations

By learning to record our visualizations and to state these clarified images in the form of affirmations, we move toward creating greater rewards and happiness in our lives.

Using this type of entry, you will write about those things you cannot actually see, but through your own imagination and mind's eye, believe or want to believe. For some, affirmations and visualizations are natural ways to move through the world. For others, asking to believe without proof or knowledge gained through the senses, is a considerable challenge. If you have not used them before, affirmations and visualizations will be worth learning.

By definition, an affirmation is a positive statement that reflects a held belief or a belief you would like to hold. It is frequently stated in first person singular beginning with your own name.

Cindy had struggled with relationships for many years. She recognized a pattern of attracting men who were not suitable for her. Her affirmation stated what she wanted, clearly and simply:

I, Cindy, attract healthy men who are loving and kind.

At first, Cindy had much resistance to her affirmation. She wanted to believe it, but she was not ready to accept her ability to attract healthy people into her life. Cindy had to first accept her negative responses. She did so like this:

I, Cindy, attract healthy men who who are loving and kind.	*Oh, right. Then what about that creep you're going out with?*
I, Cindy, attract healthy men who who are loving and kind.	*I can't change the kind of men I attract!*
I, Cindy, attract healthy men who who are loving and kind.	*Oh, please, just leave me alone!*

I, Cindy, attract healthy men who who are loving and kind.

When is this supposed to happen?

I, Cindy, attract healthy men who who are loving and kind.

Hmmm.....

I, Cindy, attract healthy men who who are loving and kind.

We'll see...

Cindy continued writing out both her affirmation and the negative responses. Soon, the negative responses became neutral and finally positive and supportive of her affirmation. Once Cindy had released her negative beliefs, she continued writing her positive affirmation. The writing and repetition of her affirmation eventually changed her outcome. Cindy began to truly attract healthy, loving and kind men into her life.

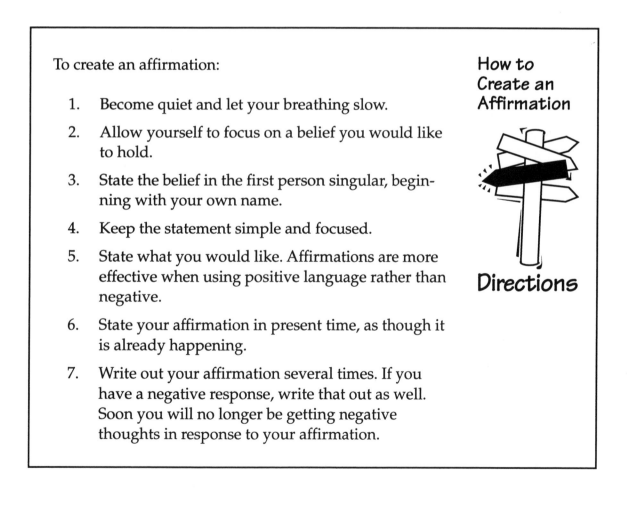

To create an affirmation:

1. Become quiet and let your breathing slow.

2. Allow yourself to focus on a belief you would like to hold.

3. State the belief in the first person singular, beginning with your own name.

4. Keep the statement simple and focused.

5. State what you would like. Affirmations are more effective when using positive language rather than negative.

6. State your affirmation in present time, as though it is already happening.

7. Write out your affirmation several times. If you have a negative response, write that out as well. Soon you will no longer be getting negative thoughts in response to your affirmation.

How to Create an Affirmation

Directions

A visualization is a picture you imagine in your mind's eye. It can be a picture of something or somewhere you have already seen or been. Or it can be an imagined picture of something you would like to see. The more details your picture contains, the more real you can make it become for yourself.

Nancy was an accomplished public speaker. She was frequently asked to present at conferences and meetings as a motivational speaker. To prepare for her talks, Nancy used visualization.

For several days before her presentation, she would spend a few minutes alone and quiet, with her eyes closed. She would see herself walking up to the podium, smiling at the audience. She would see herself calm and relaxed. She would see herself interacting with the audience and their warm and receptive response to her remarks.

When Nancy had a very complete picture of herself with all of the details in place, she would quickly write down the entire scenario. Each time she stopped to review her visualization, she had a complete visual description of what she wanted. Writing helped clarify and focus Nancy's visualization.

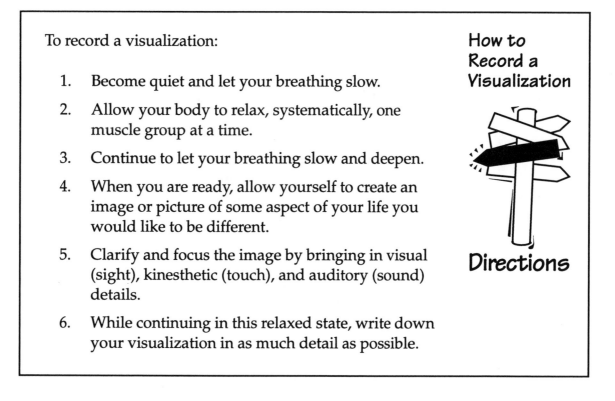

To record a visualization:

1. Become quiet and let your breathing slow.

2. Allow your body to relax, systematically, one muscle group at a time.

3. Continue to let your breathing slow and deepen.

4. When you are ready, allow yourself to create an image or picture of some aspect of your life you would like to be different.

5. Clarify and focus the image by bringing in visual (sight), kinesthetic (touch), and auditory (sound) details.

6. While continuing in this relaxed state, write down your visualization in as much detail as possible.

How to Record a Visualization

Directions

Letter Writing...An Ancient Art Revisited

The art of letter writing no longer holds an exalted place as a literary style. However, the psychological benefits of letter writing are tremendous. Some letters need to be written and never mailed, their impact far greater on the writer than the intended recipient.

To write a letter with therapeutic value, begin by writing an unedited letter to someone with whom you have unfinished business. This is not the time to be polite or socially correct. Just write the letter you really would like to write. Later, you can decide whether or not you want to edit, modify, or even send the letter.

Daniel wrote the following letter to his mother.

Dear Margaret:

I guess technically, I should call you "Mom," but since you weren't much of a mother to me, it doesn't seem right. I've been thinking about writing for a long time but I just get so mad when I think of all the times you weren't there...everything you've missed in my life. I think I'm writing now because I have a son about the age I was when you left. Somehow it seems important to say now what I need to say. I need to get some things off my chest. I'm tired of being mad at you.

When I look at my own child, I can't believe how much I love him. How you could have left me and made so little contact all of these years. Didn't you love me? For a long time I thought it was me...something I did that made you go away. Do you know what that's like, being six years old and feeling responsible for something so big?

Oh sure, you sent an occasional check and the annual Christmas gift. You called every now and again. But couldn't you at least remember my birthday? All those years, without any real contact.

Luckily, Dad married again, and Libby, his new wife, has been a real mom to me. A real mom isn't about biology, it's about being there. It's about soccer games and trick or treating on Halloween, parent nights and band concerts. She listened when kids made fun of me and when I thought no girl would ever go out with me, let alone fall in love with me. I know Libby loves me like her own son...I don't know if you even like me.

When I started to write this I felt angry, the anger of over twenty-five years. But now I feel sad. Sad for what I didn't have, sad for my son's (your grandson's loss). But mostly, I am sad for your loss.

Sincerely,
Daniel

Daniel, in fact, never sent the letter to his mother. The healing he needed to happen occurred in the process of writing the therapeutic letter.

To write a therapeutic letter:

How to Write a Therapeutic Letter

1. Become quiet and let your breathing slow.

2. Allow yourself a vision of the person you would like to write to.

3. Remember the recipient of your letter does not need to be alive.

4. When you are ready, write out all the thoughts, feelings and emotions you would like to express. Do not edit in any way.

5. Put the letter aside for at least a day or two.

6. Look at the letter again. Decide if you would like to edit or modify it. You need do nothing else. It is perfectly fine (and frequently a good choice) to not send the letter at all.

Directions

Fran and **Bob** decided to use Mutual Letter Writing. Both were shy and not very verbal in expressing their feelings. They used letter writing to express the things they wanted to say to one another but had difficulty stating in person. Once they both wrote and read what they felt, they had "broken the ice" for further discussion.

Using Art and Music...Adapting the Fine Arts

We don't necessarily think of using art and music as part of our daily journal writing practice. Yet by integrating art and music in the process of journal work, you can add depth and dimension to your entries.

If you are considering using art in your journal on a regular basis, you will want to take that into consideration when selecting the type of journal you will use.

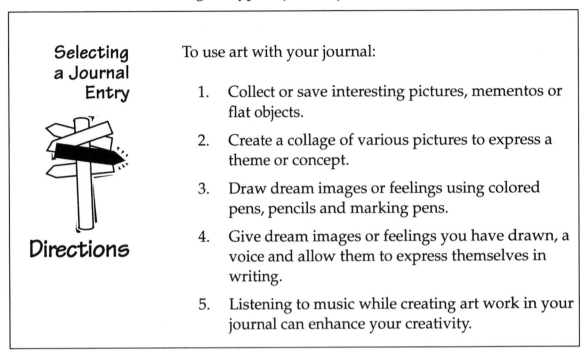

Selecting a Journal Entry

Directions

To use art with your journal:

1. Collect or save interesting pictures, mementos or flat objects.

2. Create a collage of various pictures to express a theme or concept.

3. Draw dream images or feelings using colored pens, pencils and marking pens.

4. Give dream images or feelings you have drawn, a voice and allow them to express themselves in writing.

5. Listening to music while creating art work in your journal can enhance your creativity.

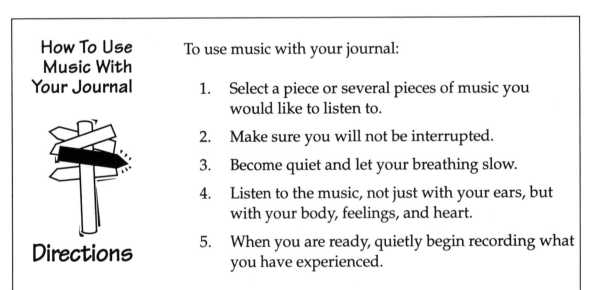

How To Use Music With Your Journal

Directions

To use music with your journal:

1. Select a piece or several pieces of music you would like to listen to.

2. Make sure you will not be interrupted.

3. Become quiet and let your breathing slow.

4. Listen to the music, not just with your ears, but with your body, feelings, and heart.

5. When you are ready, quietly begin recording what you have experienced.

The Call of Nature

Nature is another area we don't usually associate with journal writing. Bring your journal off the busy freeway of your life into the quieter path of nature. Recording while in nature will help you to regain perspective and balance.

To use your journal in nature:

How to Use Your Journal in Nature

1. Arrange for uninterrupted time at the beach, take a hike, or a walk.

2. Go alone or be silent with a partner.

3. Do not rush.

4. Pay attention to all your senses. What do you see? What do you hear? What do you feel? What do you smell? What do you taste?

5. Sit for awhile and allow thoughts and feelings to come to you. Write down what comes.

Directions

6. Notice the big picture of the landscape or terrain.

7. Notice the small perspective as well. Focus on an ant hill, the pace of a snail, the size of a grain of sand.

Continuing the Journey...

You now have the basic maps to begin your journey.

You have learned many techniques, methods, and guidelines for using your journal.

In the following three chapters, you will find even more ideas for new entries, ways to avoid pitfalls, and resources for your journal work.

Chapter Twelve

Keep Moving: 101 Ideas to Jump Start Your Journal Writing

To keep a lamp burning, we have to keep putting oil in it.
Mother Teresa

There may be days on your journey of discovery when you simply run out of ideas, when all of the methods and techniques you have learned and discovered just don't seem like enough to keep or hold your interest. One or two days like that are fine. You need to pull back from your regular activities and take a little break. However, if one or two days with no journal writing lead to more days, and then a week, then a month, you have lost the rhythm necessary for progress.

This chapter is designed to help you jump start when you're in a stuck place. You can use it to re-motivate yourself. You can play with a new method or style of entry. You can even use these ideas for three full months of journal writing entries. Or you can simply intersperse them with your regular journal keeping practice.

These are quick and easy ideas. Go in order and write straight through or skip around. Do remember, however, to have fun!

1 Write as many reasons as you can think of about why you can't, don't want to, or won't write in your journal.

2 Create an "I Want" list. Begin with the kernel sentence "I want" and write whatever comes up for you.

3 Make a list of all the things you are angry about in your life right now.

4 Make a list of all the people you appreciate.

5 Write a letter to someone you love. Decide later if you want to mail it or not.

6 What is the saddest thing you have seen or heard this week? Write about it.

7 What made you laugh the hardest this week? Write about it.

8 Like a good mystery? Write down three things that seem like total mysteries to you. Explore these three things further.

9 Write an advertisement for yourself. Discuss all your best virtues.

10 What is the oldest memory you have about your life? Write it out in as much detail as possible.

11 Think of a role model who has been important to you. What most influenced you about this person?

12 Go to a mall or big shopping area today. Write down everything you see and experience.

13 Describe your ideal intimate relationship.

14 What is the happiest thing that has ever happened in your life? Write about it.

15 Make a list of all the people in your life from whom you need to ask forgiveness.

16 Make a list of things you would like to forgive in yourself.

17 Drive or travel to your favorite nearby city or to a special area or neighborhood in your town. Pretend you are a travel guide. Describe all the points of interest and wonderful things to do.

18 Today, experiment with a new form of Free Form Writing. Pick a word, any word, and write about it for 10 minutes without stopping. If you get stuck, write down that you are stuck, but keep writing.

19 Write down all the things you did today (or yesterday if it's early in the morning). Close your eyes. Use your visual memory to record details.

20 Describe the most important phone call you ever got, one that changed your life. Describe your feelings about it.

21 Starting today, keep track of everything you eat and drink, the quantities and time you ate. Keep recording for seven days.

22 Go to an art/photography museum or exhibit. What questions would you like to ask the artist? Create a dialogue with the artist.

23 Record a dream from last night. Write out everything you remember. Have all the important players and objects speak in their own voices.

24 If you could go anywhere you wanted in the entire world, what country would you want to visit? Why? What would you want to do there?

25 Imagine going on a huge shopping spree. You could buy anything you wanted. What would you get? Why?

26 Imagine your ideal house or living space. Describe it.

27 Have you ever had a hunch, feeling or awareness something was going to happen and it did? Write 2-3 paragraphs about it.

28 Check back on your food/drink log for the entire week. What did you discover?

29 Have a dialogue with your body. Talk to it about your general state of health.

30 Congratulations! You've been keeping your journal for a month. Decide now if you're using the right journal for you. If not, treat yourself to a new one.

31 Notice where you have been writing in your journal. Do you like it there? If you do, go back to it and write any entry you choose while sitting there. If you prefer, try a new place for today.

32 Make this a Free Day! Try Free Form Writing. Remember spelling, grammar and sentence structure don't count.

33 Write down all the things you did today (or yesterday, if it's early in the morning). Close your eyes, use your auditory memory to record details.

34 Create a list of the people with whom you have unfinished business. You can dialogue with them later. For now, just begin the list.

35 Begin a project log today. Write down how far you got and how you feel about a new project you're working on.

36 Plan your ideal vacation. Where would you go? Write out the itinerary.

37 Select a room in your house you would like to re-decorate or change in some way. Sit quietly in the room. Ask it what it wants to have done or what it needs. Give the room a voice.

38 Write a movie title and short description of a plot that most clearly represents the story of your life.

39 What famous person in history would you like to meet? Why?

40 If you were an animal, what animal would you be? Why?

41 Go back to your list of people with whom you have unfinished business. Choose one person and create a dialogue.

42 What book has influenced you most in your life? Why?

43 Plan a big party for yourself. What would be the theme? Who would you invite? Why?

44 Dialogue with your "Inner Child" today.

45 If you were a flower, tree, or plant, what kind would you be? Why?

46 Pretend it's Halloween. If you could wear a costume representing any person or entity, who or what would it be? Why?

47 Consider this quotation: *"Solutions may be simple but they're seldom easy."* (B.H. Tyler) Write what it means to you.

48 Write an entry about why you don't want to write an entry today. Don't spend more than a few minutes on this. Take off and enjoy your day!

49 Take a ride in a boat or visualize a boat ride. What lessons can you learn from going with the flow?

50 Create a cartoon about something in your life that amuses you.

51 Use this today or save it for a grumpy day. Make a list of all the reasons you didn't want to get up this morning.

52 You are getting ready to write your autobiography. What would this great book be called? How would it be illustrated?

53 Keep a log of how you spend your time. Write down every time you change activities. Do this three or more days.

54 If you could be anywhere you wanted to be right now, where would it be? Say more...

55 Write a poem for today. Remember a poem doesn't have to rhyme. Focus on images and feelings.

56 Draw your family. Write down what you notice about the picture you have drawn. What would you like to change about this picture?

57 Look at your time log for the last 3 days. What did you learn about how you spend your time?

58 Recall the last beautiful sunset you saw. Describe it. Now describe the feelings you had at the time.

59 Write a letter to someone in a future generation.

60 Make an "I want" list in a different form. Draw a mind map, instead. First, draw a circle in the middle of a piece of paper. Write "I want" in the middle of the circle. Attach lines to your circle. Let each line be a wish, desire or fantasy.

61 Today, write about prosperity. Write down all the ways you can think of to be prosperous. See how many of your ideas go beyond having money.

62 Do you have an ache, pain or symptom that seems to keep reappearing? Dialogue with it now.

63 Nature day. Try a walk in nature. Bring your journal along. Write about what you experience on your walk.

64 Read any good books lately? Take a novel you have been reading or one you have finished. Write the ending you would have preferred.

65 Describe your first car or bicycle. How did your first solo ride feel?

66 Draw an abstract representation of a nagging concern that has been bothering you. Give your drawing a voice. Let it speak to you and write down what it says.

67 Happy Valentine's Day! Write your own version of "How do I love thee, let me count the ways." Make a list of all the positive things you can think of about yourself. (This is your own personal journal, it's okay to brag.)

68 Have a dialogue on paper with a historical figure you have always admired or respected.

69 Of the many roles you fulfill on a daily basis, select two that appear to be in the most conflict. Set up a dialogue between them.

70 Write down all the things you did today (or yesterday, if it's early in the morning.) Close your eyes, use your sense of smell to record details.

71 Happy April Fool's Day! Write about one of the most foolish things you have ever done. Explain its impact, if any, on your life.

72 Select a quote that has been an inspiration to you. Comment on how it has affected your life.

73 Find a tree, plant or a rock to sit near. Blocking out everything around you, become the object or living thing you are looking at. What do you imagine you would feel like?

74 What gives you a natural high? (Please do not include drugs or alcohol.) Create that experience or a reasonable facsimile in the next few days or so. Write about what happened.

75 Remember a very important event in your life that happened a long time ago. Be a reporter and write about the event from an objective perspective.

76 Describe your fantasy hideout. Make your sanctuary your own private fantasy island.

77 Music Day. Listen to your favorite music while writing for today. Listen, notice, feel what comes up for you.

78 What teacher did you like most in school? Describe what you learned from him or her.

79 If money were no object, what kind of store, shop, restaurant or establishment would you like to own. What product or service would you sell?

80 Sit near a small stream or brook today. If you don't have one near by, find a park to sit in. Become quiet and notice what feelings and thoughts come up for you.

81 Find an old photograph...what memories does it bring up for you? Write them down.

82 Write a letter to God, a spiritual guide or the Universe. Ask a question you have always wanted answered. Pay attention in the next several days (maybe your question will be answered).

83 Go to a coffee house or restaurant alone. Take your journal. Write about what you see, and feel going on around you. Notice what's going on inside of you.

84 Examine a piece of fruit. Look at it very closely. What do you notice about it. Very slowly, begin to open it, cut into pieces, take it apart. What do you see, smell, hear, taste and feel?

85 Select two aspects of your personality that appear to be in conflict. Set up a dialogue between them.

86 Make an appointment to have body work or a massage. Leave lots of time to follow. Take a short nap, meditate or just spend some quiet time. Write an entry about how you feel.

87 Write down all the things you did today (or yesterday, if it's early in the morning). Close your eyes, use your kinesthetic memory to record details.

88 Happy Thanksgiving! Even if this isn't Thanksgiving Day, what in your life are you most thankful for?

89 Write down three things you wish your parents would have done differently. Explore the impact this would have had on your life.

90 Purposely, do not write in your journal for today. Notice how you feel without writing about it.

91 Write about how it felt to not write yesterday.

92 Get a package of crayons or marking pens. Close your eyes and get in touch with your feelings. Quickly, giving yourself only a minute, draw whatever comes up for you. Give your drawing a voice. Write down what it says to you.

93 Happy holiday! Describe the best gift you could give yourself.

94 Make up a holiday. Give it a name and describe how you would like to celebrate.

95 What is your favorite fairy tale? What character do you relate to? Why?

96 Take a bus that you seldom or never take. Take your journal. Observe what you feel and notice. (If you usually take the bus to get around, try the train or other form of local transportation.)

97 Write a newspaper front page with your day's events as headlines.

98 Gather together some art materials. Create a mask that represents the face you show most often to the world. Then create a mask that represents your inner, private world.

99 Write your own obituary. What would you like to be remembered for?

100 Who is the "Wind beneath your wings?" Write him or her a thank you letter.

101 Today, practice a "random act of kindness." Write about how it made you feel.

Chapter Thirteen

Avoiding Detours...Answers to Your Questions Before You Ask Them

If we would have new knowledge, we must have a whole world of new questions.
Susan K. Langer

If you have questions about things you have read or entries you have tried, you're on the right track. I've taken the liberty of anticipating your questions from the first two sections of the book.

Most of the questions and answers presented here are questions I have been asked during or after journal workshops.

If, however, you have no questions, that's fine too. Get back to your journal and start writing!

Q. I'd love to keep a journal, but I'm worried someone will read what I've written and they will become upset or angry with me. What should I do?

A. A journal is designed as a private type of writing. It is not written with the intention to share. If someone reads something you have written that you did not intend for them to read, you really need not take responsibility for them. Reasonable caution suggests that your journal be stored in an out-of-the-way place, or put with private papers or other personal items. Occasionally people worry their journal will be used against them or cause them some sort of harm. On very rare occasions, journals have been used in a court of law as evidence.

However, as a journal writer, you will have to make a choice between the tremendous benefits of keeping a journal and the unlikely possibility writing in your journal will cause you harm. If you do have concerns, however, here are three suggestions. You might choose to lock your journal in a drawer, desk or briefcase. You might write your journal on a computer and store it in a locked file. Finally, you might write a disclaimer in the front of your journal, stating the journal is your private property and contains your private thoughts.

Q. Are there particular writing "rituals" that would make it easier to write on a regular basis?

A. Yes. Remember a favorite chair you sat in while you studied? Creating a particular physical space on a habitual basis helps promote the desire to write on a regular basis. Have your journal and a special pen set aside for writing time. Try to write daily. Like exercise, you will find you achieve the best progress when you write on a regular basis. Early morning and evenings are both good times. Making a cup of tea, playing music you enjoy and becoming quiet before you write are the type of rituals you might want to create. As in all your journal writing practices, find rituals that nurture and support you.

Q. It seems like I only write when I'm depressed. Any suggestions?

A. I am frequently asked this question. My suggestion is that you write everyday to break the pattern of writing only when you're depressed. Even one or two sentences may soon get you out of the rut. If you start writing, you are likely to write more than one sentence. You'll begin to see subtle changes as you use your journal on a regular basis. Writing with regularity will not only release the pattern of writing only when depressed, it will help with depression in general.

Q. I used to keep a journal, but now I've stopped writing altogether. How do I get started again?

A. This reminds me of the Nike slogan, "Just do it." Just start. Don't even make a commitment to write more than that first day back. You might want to begin your entry with "It's been a long time since I wrote..." Now keep going. Write how you feel about not writing. Write what you've been doing since you last wrote. Write about the fears you had about starting to write again. You may find you have so much to say you'll want to continue tomorrow!

Q. I received a beautiful bound journal as a gift. I feel silly, but I don't want to write in it. It's too "nice" to write in? Should I get a new journal to use?

A. Of course you can get a new journal if you want one. What I like to do when I have a new journal, especially a "pretty" one, is start right out with an opening sentence like, "I'm afraid I'll mess up this new journal." There, you did it.

Q. Could you go over the "Dialogue" entries again? I'm not sure how to get started with a dialogue.

A. Remember the dialogue is used to bring together alienated parts of the self or unfinished business with others. Begin by finding the core conflict. Is the struggle within yourself or with others? Is it an issue that feels unfinished or incomplete? Is it a thought or a feeling that needs to be stated? Set your dialogue up as though you were writing a screen play. The conflicted parts or unfinished work are your characters. Be conversational. Let your characters speak for themselves.

Q. I'm fine getting started with the dialogue, but I get stuck half way through.

A. This is a common concern. It may be you were lacking in clarity before you started or you lost focus once you began to write. Stop for a minute. Close your eyes. Get a picture of the person you are in dialogue with. If you are dialoguing with yourself, get a picture of that role or part of your personality. Feel the feelings that part or person has. Hear the voice they would be speaking from. This same method will work with any type of dialogue.

Q. Maybe I'm an exhibitionist, but I sometimes want to show people what I've written in my journal. Is there any *danger* in that?

A. Not if you do it very carefully and are clear about your intention. Sometimes I've written an entry that describes so clearly what I'm thinking or feeling that I choose to share it in a selective way. It's frequently appropriate to do this if you are in regular on-going therapy. However remember to always honor yourself first in your journal writing and never to share what doesn't feel right to share.

Q. I've tried keeping a journal and find it's just not my "thing." Any other ideas?

A. It's entirely possible journal writing is simply not for you. You might try combining journal writing with art, taking a nature walk, or writing after body work or meditation. If you've tried journal writing and none of the suggestions work for you, just let go of it. Simply ask yourself what you would rather be doing instead and do that. I have also found that as we grow and change in our lives our interests and needs change as well. Put your journal aside for now. There may be another time in your life when journaling will work for you.

Q. Do I have to write everyday?

A. No. Some people write every day. Some write every other day, some less frequently. Just as you listen to your body to tell you how often to exercise, listen to your inner voice to tell you how frequently to write. Some days you may feel like writing for several minutes or even hours. Some days you will not feel like writing at all. Try writing a few sentences or for five minutes without a break. If that still doesn't feel right, honor your own needs.

Q. I've been writing in a journal for years. It's all beginning to sound the same. How do I get out of the rut?

A. First of all, make sure you are indicating the date (including year) and time noting your entries or it may very likely begin to sound the same. Schedule some time to re-read some of your journals. Look for patterns and subtle changes from season to season and year to year. I think you will begin to see more patterns than ruts. Write about the patterns you observe. Ask yourself questions about what's keeping you stuck, what's blocking you and what you would like to happen differently. Responding to your own questions in this way is likely to move you forward.

Q. My schedule is absolutely jammed. How can I fit in journal writing?

A. The same way you fit in everything else. Schedule it. Put a note in your personal calendar and treat your journal writing time like an appointment with someone very important! Remember, writing only five or ten minutes daily can be even more useful than writing for long stretches at a time.

Q. I've heard journal writing can help me solve personal problems, but how can just writing things down really solve anything?

A. That's a good question. The answer seems to lie in the process of writing itself and in releasing feelings. For many people, writing provides an outlet similar to what Freud referred to as the "talking cure." Writing out a problem helps clarify the situation, expand your awareness and provide you with options you had not been aware of before. With expanded options you have greater flexibility to problem solve.

Q. Why do I need a special journal? Won't just any notebook do?

A. Absolutely. However, a special journal helps with motivation. It's simply more fun to have a journal. If you have positive feelings about the journal itself, you are more likely to use it.

Q. Sometimes my journal feels more like a day-to-day reporting log? How can I make it more interesting?

A. Re-read the chapter 4, "Beyond Dear Diary." Increase the depth of your diary log by bringing in sensory awareness (smells, sights, sounds, textures). As you write, deepen your consciousness by asking yourself questions like: "What else might this mean for me? What else can I find out about myself?" Finally, you can write out the ongoing internal monologue that happens as you write about events in a reporting style. These methods will add interest to your day-to-day entries.

Q. Should I take a journal with me when I travel?

A. Definitely! Traveling with your journal can enrich the power of your observations. It can add colorful detail to descriptions, help guide your decision-making if you feel lost or confused, and generally serve as a travel companion who won't argue with you. When you make entries in your journal away from home, be sure to write down the date and time as well as the place. This makes a great travelogue once you get home.

Q. I love writing letters, but I can't seem to start a journal. I feel like my letters are my journal. Any ideas?

 A. I love writing in my journal yet I infrequently write letters. I believe the two processes are very much related. They are both a written version of your inner thoughts, feelings and actions. If you prefer writing letters, try copying them and putting them in your journal. You deserve to receive a letter from yourself, too!

 Q. Isn't it better to write when I'm by myself? What's the point of writing with others around?

 A. Journal writing is essentially a private process. However many journal keepers enjoy writing in small groups or workshops. Having others around you who are writing at the same time can feel very supportive. Remember to respect your own needs in terms of privacy and sharing.

Q. I spend hours commuting. Is there anyway to incorporate the methods you suggest while driving?

A. Yes. Keep a micro tape recorder with you. If you get a brilliant idea or insight, note the day and time and record it on tape. You will, however, need to allow time to transcribe what you have written.

Q. I get the best thoughts for my journal while walking and in the shower. By the time I get to write them down, they're gone. Any thoughts?

A. I have paper and a pen in every room of my home as well as in my car. You never know when you'll want to record a thought. Try tucking a small tablet of paper and a pen in your pocket before you start on your walk. Keep paper and a pen or a small tape recorder in the bathroom.

Q. I think better and faster writing with a word processor. Can I keep a journal on my computer?

A. Certainly. The word processor is a great way to keep a journal. Many people can write and think faster in this way. If you would like to keep your journal in a more traditional way as well, you can simply make a hard copy of what you wrote in the computer and then add it to your journal.

Q. What do you think about listening to music while writing? I notice that it calms me down.

A. Do whatever works best for you. Creating a mood with music is a good way to center yourself before writing. You might even experiment with different types of music and see what comes up for you. Also, there are many good relaxation and meditation tapes out as well.

Q. I'm exhausted at night. I take out my journal to write and fall asleep before I can even finish the first paragraph. Help!

A. Listen to your body! You may simply not be getting enough sleep or you may be a morning person who would do better writing in the morning rather than at night. Experiment a little. Try writing at different times of the day and notice what works best for you. Again, whenever you choose to write in your journal, a small amount of writing is perfectly fine.

Q. I'd like to share my journal with my granddaughter when she's a little older. Is that a good idea?

A. It's a great idea. I suggest however, you write as freely as possible and edit later. You can then get the full pleasure and benefit of your journal keeping for you and have the gift of sharing it with your grandchild.

Chapter Fourteen

Guidebooks for the Journey

Fitting people with books is about as difficult as fitting them with shoes.

Sylvia Beach

In my experience of almost two decades of teaching the journal writing process, I have found a high correlation between people who like to write and people who like to read. Known to my clients and workshop participants as a bibliotherapist, this chapter offers over seventy-five additional books to support and expand the concepts in *Writing From the Inside Out*.

Since thousands of books are published each year, this list is only a sampling. Please let me know about your favorites for future editions.

Other Books on Journal Writing

Adams, Kathleen, *Journal to the Self: Twenty-Two Paths to Personal Growth.* New York: Warner Books, Inc., 1990.

Baldwin, Christina, *Life's Companion: Journal Writing as a Spiritual Quest.* New York: Bantam, 1991.

Baldwin, Christina, *One to One: Self-Understanding Through Journal Writing.* New York: M. Evans and Co., 1977.

Borkin, Susan L., *Journal Writing as Self-Therapy.* (Unpublished masters thesis). San Francisco, California: Lone Mountain College, 1978.

Casewit, Curtis W., *The Diary: A Complete Guide to Journal Writing.* Allen, Texas: Argus Communications, 1982.

Johnson, Dan, *Creative Guide to Journal Writing: How to Enrich Your Life With a Written Journal.* Louisville, Colorado: Gateway Publications, 1989.

Hagan, Kay Leigh, *Internal Affairs: A Journalkeeping Workbook for Self-Intimacy.* New York: HarperCollins, 1988.

Progoff, Ira, *At a Journal Workshop (Writing to Access the Power of Unconscious and Evoke Creative Ability).* Los Angeles: J.P. Tarcher, 1992.

Rainer, Tristine, *The New Diary: How to Use a Journal for Self-Guidance and Expanded Creativity.* Los Angeles, California: J.P. Tarcher, 1978.

Selling, Bernard, *Writing From Within: A Step-By-Step Guide to Writing Your Life's Stories.* Claremont, California: Hunter House, Inc., 1988.

Simons, George, *Keeping Your Personal Journal.* New York: Paulist Press, 1978.

Affirmations and Visualization

Gawain, Shakti, *Creative Visualization.* New York: Bantam, 1979.

Hay, Louise, *You Can Heal Your Life.* Santa Monica: Hay House, 1987.

Ray, Sondra, *I Deserve Love.* Berkeley, California: Celestial Arts, 1976.

Roman, Sanaya and Duane Packer, *Creating Money: Keys to Abundance.* Tiburon: H J Kramer, Inc., 1988.

Art Therapy

Capacchione, Lucia, *The Creative Journal: The Art of Finding Yourself.* Athens, Ohio: Swallow Press, 1979.

Capacchione, Lucia, *The Picture of Health: Healing Your Life With Art.* Santa Monica, California: Hay House, 1990.

Capacchione, Lucia, *The Well-Being Journal: Drawing on Your Inner Power to Heal Yourself.* North Hollywood, California: Newcastle Publishing Co., Inc., 1989.

Creativity and Mind Mapping

Ballenger, Bruce and Barry Lane, *Discovering the Writer Within: 40 Days to More Imaginative Writing.* Cincinnati, Ohio: Writer's Digest Books, 1989.

Bryant, Jean, *Anybody Can Write: A Playful Approach.* San Rafael, California: New World Library, 1985.

Capacchione, Lucia, *The Power of Your Other Hand.* North Hollywood, California: Newcastle Publishing Co., Inc., 1988.

Goldberg, Natalie, *Wild Mind.* New York: Bantam Books, 1990.

Goldberg, Natalie, *Writing Down the Bones: Freeing the Writer Within.* Boston, Massachusetts: Shambhala Publications, Inc., 1986.

Hughes-Calero, Heather, *Writing as a Tool for Self-Discovery.* Carmel, California: Coastline Publishing Company, 1988.

Klauser, Henriette Anne, *Writing on Both Sides of the Brain: Breakthrough Techniques for People Who Write.* New York: HarperCollins, 1987.

Metzger, Deena, *Writing for Your Life: A Guide and Companion to Your Inner Life.* San Francisco: HarperSanFrancisco, 1992.

Rico, Gabriele Lusser, *Pain and Possibility: Writing Your Way Through Personal Crisis.* Los Angeles: J.P. Tarcher, Inc., 1991.

Rico, Gabriele Lusser, *Writing the Natural Way: Using Right Brain Techniques to Release Your Expressive Powers.* Los Angeles: J.P. Tarcher, Inc., 1983.

Ross, Elizabeth Irvin, *How to Write While You Sleep: And Other Surprising Ways to Increase Your Writing Power.* Cincinnati, Ohio: Writer's Digest Books, 1985.

Thornburg, David, *Unlocking Personal Creativity: A Course in Idea Mapping.* Los Altos, California: Starson Publications, 1986.

Diarists and Diary Collections

Cahill, Susan (Ed.), *Writing Women's Lives.* New York: HarperCollins, 1994.

Culley, Margo, (Ed.), *A Day at a Time: The Diary Literature of American Women from 1764 to the Present.* New York: City University of New York, The Feminist Press, 1985.

Moffat, Mary Jane and Charlotte Painter, (Ed.) *Revelations: Diaries of Women.* New York: Vintage Books, 1974.

Nin, Anais, *The Diary of Anais Nin.* New York: Swallow Press and Harcourt, Brace and World, Inc., 1966-1974.

Sarton, May, *After the Stroke.* New York: W.W. Norton, 1988.

Sarton, May, *At Seventy: A Journal.* New York: W.W. Norton, 1984.

Sarton, May, *Journal of a Solitude.* New York: Norton, 1973.

Dreams

Farady, Ann, *Dream Power.* New York: Berkeley, 1972.

Foreman, Ellen, *Awakening: A Dream Journal,* New York: Stewart, Tabori & Chang, 1988.

Garfield, Patricia, *Creative Dreaming.* New York: Ballantine, 1974.

Ullman, Montague and Nan Zimmerman, *Working With Dreams.* J. P. Tarcher, Inc., 1979.

Wild, Laynee, *The Complete Dream Journal.* San Francisco: Pomegranate, 1994.

Gestalt Therapy

Latner, Joel, *The Gestalt Therapy Book.* New York: Bantam, 1973.

Polster, Miriam and Erving, *Gestalt Therapy Integrated: Contours of Theory and Practice.* New York: Vintage Books, 1974.

Simkin, James S. Ph.D., *Gestalt Therapy Mini-lectures.* Millbrae, California: Celestial Arts, 1976.

Grief and Loss

Edelman, Hope, *Motherless Daughters: The Legacy of Loss.* Reading, Massachusetts: Addison-Wesley, 1994.

Kubler-Ross, Elisabeth, M.D., *On Death and Dying.* New York: Collier, 1970.

Tattlebaum, Judy, *The Courage to Grief.* New York: Lippincott and Crowell, 1980.

Tattlebaum, Judy, *You Don't Have to Suffer: A Handbook for Moving Beyond Life's Crises.* New York: Harper and Row, 1989.

Inspirational Journals

Hagan, Kay Leigh, *Prayers to the Moon.* San Francisco: HarperSanFrancisco, 1991.

Hay, Louise, *A Garden of Thoughts.* Santa Monica, California: Hay House, 1989.

Yarrow, Ruth, *Journal for Reflections.* Freedom, California: The Crossing Press, 1988.

The Diarist's Journal. Philadelphia: Running Press, 1988.

Dream Journal: A Diary of Inner Visions. Philadelphia: Running Press, 1988.

Talking to Myself. Center City, Minnesota: Hazelden, 1992.

Recovery

Bass, Ellen and Laura Davis, *The Courage to Heal: A Guide For Women Survivors of Sexual Abuse.* New York: Harper and Row, 1988.

Foster, Carolyn, *The Family Patterns Workbook: Breaking Free From Your Past and Creating a Life of Your Own.* New York: Jeremy P. Tarcher/Perigee books, 1993.

Solly, Richard and Roseann Lloyd, *Journey Notes: Writing for Recovery and Spiritual Growth.* New York: Ballantine (Hazelden), 1989.

Stepping Stones: A Journal. Minneapolis, Minnesota: CompCare, 1985.

The Twelve Steps for Everyone Who Really Wants Them. Minneapolis, Minnesota: CompCare, 1975.

Solitude

Halpern, Sue, *Migrations to Solitude.* New York: Pantheon Books, 1992.

Storr, Anthony, *Solitude: A Return to the Self,* New York: Ballantine, 1988.

Teens/Family Growth

Bingham, Mindy and Judy Edmondson and Sandy Stryker, *Choices: A Teen Woman's Journal for Self-Awareness and Personal Planning.* Santa Barbara, California: Advocacy Press, 1983.

Stillman, Peter, *Families Writing.* Cincinnati, Ohio: Writer's Digest Books, 1989.

Weight Issues

Hirschmann, Jane and Carol Munter, *Overcoming Overeating.* New York: Ballantine, 1988.

Orbach, Susie, *Fat is a Feminist Issue.* New York: Berkeley, 1978.

Roth, Geneen, *When Food is Love: Exploring the Relationship Between Eating and Intimacy.* New York: Dutton, 1991.

Roth, Geneen, *Why Weight? A Guide to Ending Compulsive Eating.* New York: Plume, 1989.

Wardell, Judy, *Thin Within.* New York: Harmony Books, 1985.

Waterhouse, Debra, *Outsmarting the Female Fat Cell.* New York: Hyperion, 1993.

Women's Personal and Spiritual Growth

Anderson, Sherry Ruth and Patricia Hopkins, *The Feminine Face of God: The Unfolding of the Sacred in Women.* New York: Bantam, 1991.

Field, Joanna, *A Life of One's Own.* Los Angeles: J. P. Tarcher, 1981.

King, Laurel, *Women of Power.* Berkeley, California: Celestial Arts, 1989.

Louden, Jennifer, *The Women's Comfort Book.* San Francisco: HarperSanFrancisco, 1992.

Mariechild, Diane. *A Feminist Guide to Psychic Development.* New York: The Crossing Press, 1981.

Newman, Leslea, *Writing From the Heart: Inspiration and Exercises for Women Who Want to Write.* Freedom, California: Crossing Press, 1993.

Ross, Ruth, *Prospering Woman.* Mill Valley, California: Whatever Publishing, 1982.

Snow, Kimberly, *Writing Yourself Home: A Women's Guided Journey of Self Discovery.* Emeryville, California: Conari Press, 1989.

Writers on Writing

Brande, Ueland, *Becoming a Writer.* (Originally published in 1934, reprinted with new forward.) Los Angeles: J.P. Tarcher, 1981.

Brown, Rita Mae, *Starting From Scratch: A Different Kind of Writers' Manual.* New York: Bantam, 1988.

Dillard, Annie, *The Writing Life.* New York: HarperCollins, 1989.

Lamott, Anne, *Bird by Bird: Some Instructions on Writing and Life.* New York: Pantheon, 1994.

Other Journal Writing Resources

The following resources are listed to provide you with contacts, organizations and workshops to further enhance your writing:

Authors Guild and Authors League of America
234 W. 44th street
New York, New York 10036

Feminist Women's Writing Workshops, Inc.
P.O. Box 6583
Ithaca, New York 14851

Flight of the Mind: Summer Writing Workshops for Women
622 SE 28th Avenue
Portland, Oregon 97214

International Women's Writing Guild
Box 810 Gracie Station
New York, New York 10028

Journal and Diary Enthusiasts (JADE)
1302 Washington Place
San Diego, California 92103

Poets and Writers
72 Spring Street
New York, New York 10012

Writer's Connection
P.O. Box 24770
San Jose, California 95154

Writer's Digest
1507 Dana Avenue
Cincinnati, Ohio 45207

About This Book

In faith that you will one day share with others, your thoughts and inspirations which are now only yours...

Enclosure card from gift journal, received in 1970

This book began for me with a very special and growing realization that there was a connection between the act of writing and a sense of relief and release after I had jotted down words or pounded on my typewriter. Years before the days of personal computers and user friendly word processors for the computer illiterate (ahem...) I knew instinctively that I simply felt better after I wrote down what I was feeling.

The more formal steps probably began over twenty-five years ago, the day I wrote in my journal, sitting under a tree on the small midwestern campus where I was in school:

Writing as therapy???

At the time I wrote that phrase, I didn't even know what it meant (I was, after all, only a junior, I hadn't even graduated yet). I was then an English major and a psychology minor. I sensed the intricate connection I felt between words and feelings, and that connection would prove to be a most powerful theme in my life.

I was fortunate enough to be able to use "Journal Writing as Self-Therapy" as the topic of my Master's Thesis almost twenty years ago. The Thesis itself has served as a basis for my Journal Writing for Personal Growth training workshops and presentations for hundreds of individuals.

The creation of this book from its original thesis form through dozens of training workshops has been a work in progress for over a decade. It has been a long, strenuous and growing process for me. It is in a sense, a process that reflects not only a span of many years, but serves as an ongoing evolution of the deepest part of me. The journal has been the thread that has served to keep me sewn together when it felt as though my life was coming apart at the seams. Beyond friends, intimate relationships, major lifestyle changes and deep personal loss, it has always been there. It links me to my past, my present, and I know, my future.

This book is dedicated to the hundreds of individuals I have worked with and known over the years as both a teacher and a therapist. It is dedicated to those whose stories are woven throughout these pages. And it is dedicated to those who may now begin their own journey. *Writing From the Inside Out* offers you a chance to use a journal as a tool for personal growth and transformation. I wish you a wonderful journey!

An Invitation...

To Heal Your Life and Free Your Creative Self

- ✧ Overwhelmed by a project and don't know where to begin?
- ✧ Have a thesis, dissertation or book you can't quite finish?
- ✧ Feel like you have a fabulous creative idea but don't have the time to even start it?
- ✧ Feel like you've got more to offer but don't quite know what it is?

Doing something new or finishing (and letting go) of something old can be confusing and overwhelming. *You don't have to do it alone.*

Be guided by an experienced coach with the listening skills of a psychotherapist, the practical writing skills of a published author, and the creativity of a passionate teacher.

Let Susan Borkin coach you to success by breaking through what's keeping you stuck and creating a practical step-by-step plan to achieve your heart's desire.

Based in Los Altos, California, Susan Borkin is available via phone or in person for coaching, consultation and training nationwide.

To find out more about her services, contact Susan Borkin at:

P.O. Box 1615
Los Altos, CA 94023-1615
(650) 964-3732
(650) 961-9914 (Fax)
www.susanborkin.com
E-mail: susan@susanborkin.com

Journal Writing Updates ...

Directions

To receive free updates including:

- ✦ New websites devoted to journal writing

- ✦ New books

- ✦ Seminar schedule

- ✦ Inspirational messages to keep you motivated

- ✦ For all this and more send an e-mail to…

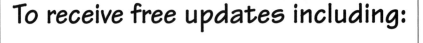

Updates@SusanBorkin.com